DYLAN FOX

Mobile App development with Concurrency

First edition

This book was professionally typeset on Reedsy.
Find out more at *reedsy.com*

Contents

Introduction to Mobile App Development and Concurrency

Overview of Mobile App Development

Mobile app development is the process of creating software applications designed to run on mobile devices such as smartphones and tablets. These applications, commonly referred to as mobile apps, are developed to provide various functionalities that enhance user experience, ranging from communication and entertainment to productivity and health tracking. The development process involves several stages, including planning, designing, coding, testing, and deployment.

Key Aspects of Mobile App Development

1. **Platform Selection**: Mobile apps can be developed for specific platforms (iOS, Android) or as cross-platform applications using frameworks like Flutter, React Native, or Xamarin. Developers choose a platform based on target audience demographics, device capabilities, and business objectives.

2. **Development Environment**: Setting up the development environment is a critical first step. For iOS, developers use Xcode with Swift or Objective-C, while Android apps are typically built using Android Studio with Java or Kotlin. Cross-platform apps may use VS Code or other Integrated Development Environments (IDEs) compatible with

1

frameworks like Flutter.

3. **Programming Languages**: The choice of programming languages is influenced by the platform:

- iOS: Swift and Objective-C
- Android: Java and Kotlin
- Cross-Platform: Dart (Flutter), JavaScript (React Native), and C# (Xamarin)

1. **App Architecture**: The architecture of a mobile app determines its structure, scalability, and maintainability. Developers often use architectural patterns such as Model-View-Controller (MVC), Model-View-ViewModel (MVVM), or Redux to manage how the app components interact and handle data.

2. **User Interface (UI) and User Experience (UX)**: Creating an engaging and intuitive UI/UX is essential in mobile app development. Developers use platform-specific design guidelines (Apple's Human Interface Guidelines for iOS and Material Design for Android) to ensure a consistent and user-friendly experience.

3. **Backend Integration**: Many mobile apps require a backend server to handle data storage, authentication, and APIs. Developers often integrate RESTful APIs or GraphQL services to enable communication between the app and the backend server.

4. **Testing and Debugging**: Mobile apps undergo rigorous testing to identify and resolve bugs, optimize performance, and ensure compatibility across different devices. Tools like XCTest for iOS, Espresso for Android, and third-party solutions like Appium for cross-platform testing help developers maintain high quality.

5. **Deployment and Maintenance**: Once developed, mobile apps are deployed to platforms like the Apple App Store or Google Play Store. Maintenance involves regular updates to introduce new features, fix bugs, and ensure compatibility with new operating system versions and device models.

Importance of Concurrency in Mobile Apps

Concurrency is crucial in mobile app development as it enables the efficient execution of multiple tasks simultaneously, improving app performance, responsiveness, and user experience. Without concurrency, apps would run sequentially, leading to delays and a poor user experience, especially when handling intensive tasks like network requests, database access, and multimedia processing.

Key Reasons for the Importance of Concurrency in Mobile Apps

1. **Enhancing App Responsiveness**:

- Concurrency ensures that long-running operations, such as network requests or database queries, do not block the main thread, which is responsible for user interface updates. By offloading these tasks to background threads, the main thread remains free to handle user interactions, resulting in a smooth and responsive app experience.

1. **Efficient Use of System Resources**:

- Mobile devices have limited resources, such as CPU and memory. Concurrency allows developers to manage these resources effectively by distributing tasks across multiple cores or threads. This helps optimize CPU usage, reduce battery consumption, and improve overall system performance.

1. **Handling Network Operations**:

- Network operations, such as fetching data from an API or uploading files, are often time-consuming and require waiting for a response. By using concurrency techniques (e.g., asynchronous programming), apps can perform these operations in the background while the user continues interacting with the app. This approach prevents UI freezing

3

and enhances the perceived speed and reliability of the app.

1. **Managing Background Tasks**:

- Many mobile apps require background tasks, such as fetching location data, downloading files, or syncing data with a server. Concurrency allows these tasks to run periodically or when specific conditions are met, without interrupting the user's activities. Background services and task schedulers (like WorkManager in Android or Background Tasks in iOS) enable developers to implement these features efficiently.

1. **Multimedia Processing**:

- Concurrency is essential for apps that involve multimedia processing, such as video editing, real-time image filtering, or audio manipulation. These tasks are computationally intensive and require significant processing power. By distributing these tasks across multiple threads, developers can ensure that multimedia features run smoothly without compromising the app's responsiveness.

1. **Improving App Scalability and Performance**:

- Apps that handle large datasets or perform complex computations benefit significantly from concurrency. Techniques like task-based concurrency and asynchronous APIs allow these operations to be broken down into smaller, manageable tasks that run concurrently. This not only improves the performance of the app but also allows it to scale efficiently as data volumes increase.

1. **Enabling Real-Time Features**:

- Concurrency is crucial for apps with real-time features, such as messaging, live updates, or location tracking. By using concurrent techniques, these apps can maintain multiple connections, handle real-time data streams, and update the UI instantly, creating a seamless and interactive experience for users.

1. **Optimizing User Experience Across Platforms**:

- Mobile platforms (iOS and Android) offer different concurrency models and APIs. Understanding and implementing concurrency using platform-specific tools like Grand Central Dispatch (GCD) and Operation Queues in iOS or Kotlin Coroutines and Executors in Android ensures that apps perform optimally on each platform. Cross-platform frameworks (e.g., Flutter, React Native) also provide concurrency support to maintain a consistent user experience.

Objectives of the Book

The primary goal of *Mobile App Development with Concurrency* is to provide developers with a comprehensive understanding of concurrency in mobile app development, enabling them to build efficient, scalable, and high-performance applications. The book covers platform-specific and cross-platform concurrency models, tools, and best practices, ensuring that readers gain practical, hands-on experience in implementing concurrency for various mobile app use cases.

Specific Objectives:

1. **Fundamentals of Concurrency**: Explain the core concepts of concurrency, including synchronous and asynchronous programming, threading, and task management, in the context of mobile app development.
2. **Platform-Specific Implementation**: Guide readers through implementing concurrency on iOS and Android using tools like Grand Central Dispatch (GCD), Operation Queues, Kotlin Coroutines, and Executors.

3. **Cross-Platform Concurrency Techniques**: Introduce concurrency methods for cross-platform frameworks like Flutter, React Native, and Xamarin, allowing developers to apply these concepts consistently across different environments.

4. **Practical Examples and Case Studies**: Provide practical examples, code snippets, and case studies that illustrate real-world applications of concurrency, such as handling network operations, multimedia processing, and managing background tasks.

5. **Performance Optimization**: Teach best practices for optimizing performance, memory usage, and battery consumption while implementing concurrent features in mobile applications.

6. **Testing and Debugging**: Offer insights into testing and debugging concurrent code, helping developers identify and resolve issues that commonly arise in multi-threaded environments.

7. **Advanced Concurrency Patterns**: Explore advanced concurrency patterns such as reactive programming, structured concurrency, and task scheduling, equipping developers with tools to build complex and efficient mobile applications.

8. **Security and Maintenance**: Emphasize the importance of secure coding practices and post-launch maintenance for apps with concurrent features, ensuring stability and long-term reliability.

Prerequisites and Audience

Prerequisites

- **Basic Programming Knowledge**: Readers should have a foundational understanding of programming languages like Java, Kotlin, Swift, JavaScript, or Dart, as these are commonly used in mobile app development.

- **Familiarity with Mobile Development**: Prior experience in developing mobile apps (either for iOS, Android, or using cross-platform frameworks) is recommended. Readers should be comfortable working with development environments like Xcode, Android Studio, or Visual Studio Code.

- **Understanding of Mobile Architecture**: A basic knowledge of mobile app architecture and UI development concepts will be beneficial as the book covers advanced topics that build upon these foundations.
- **Curiosity and Willingness to Learn**: While advanced knowledge of concurrency is not required, a willingness to explore and experiment with concurrency techniques is essential, as the book contains hands-on exercises and coding challenges.

Audience

- **Mobile App Developers**: This book is primarily targeted at mobile app developers who want to enhance their apps with efficient and scalable concurrency features.
- **Cross-Platform Developers**: Developers working with cross-platform frameworks like Flutter, React Native, and Xamarin will find value in learning how to implement consistent concurrency techniques across different platforms.
- **Intermediate to Advanced Developers**: The content is designed for developers who already have some experience with mobile development and are looking to deepen their understanding of concurrency to create more robust and high-performing applications.
- **Software Engineers and Students**: Software engineers and computer science students interested in mobile development and concurrency concepts will gain practical skills and theoretical knowledge applicable to real-world projects.

Structure and How to Use This Book

This book is structured to take readers on a step-by-step journey through the concepts and practices of concurrency in mobile app development. Each chapter builds upon the previous one, gradually increasing in complexity and covering different aspects of concurrency, from fundamentals to advanced techniques and real-world applications. The book is divided into the following sections:

1. **Fundamentals and Setup**:

- The first few chapters introduce the core concepts of mobile app development and concurrency, providing readers with a solid foundation.
- Chapters on setting up the development environment and understanding platform-specific concurrency models will help readers prepare for hands-on coding.

1. **Implementing Concurrency**:

- The middle chapters focus on practical implementation, covering threading, task management, network operations, multimedia processing, and database concurrency.
- Each chapter includes code snippets and examples to demonstrate how to apply these techniques effectively in mobile applications.

1. **Advanced Techniques and Patterns**:

- The latter chapters explore advanced concurrency topics such as reactive programming, async/await, structured concurrency, and performance optimization.
- Real-world case studies illustrate how to build complex apps with concurrent features, providing insights into scaling and optimizing performance.

1. **Testing, Debugging, and Maintenance**:

- Chapters on testing and debugging concurrent code help readers identify and resolve common issues.

- The book also covers post-launch maintenance, ensuring developers understand how to monitor and update their apps for continued stability and performance.

1. **Conclusion and Future Trends**:

- The final chapters discuss future trends in mobile concurrency, offering readers insights into emerging technologies and frameworks.
- The book concludes with a summary of key concepts and a roadmap for further learning.

How to Use This Book

- **Sequential Learning**: Readers are encouraged to follow the chapters sequentially, as each chapter builds upon the previous one. This approach is particularly beneficial for those who want to gain a comprehensive understanding of concurrency in mobile development.
- **Hands-On Practice**: Throughout the book, practical exercises, coding challenges, and case studies provide opportunities to apply learned concepts. Readers are encouraged to work through these examples and modify them to deepen their understanding.
- **Reference Guide**: The book can also serve as a reference guide for developers looking for specific information or techniques related to concurrency in mobile apps. Each chapter is structured to stand alone, allowing readers to jump directly to the topic of interest.
- **Code Repository**: A companion code repository is available online, providing all the code examples and solutions to the challenges discussed in the book. Readers can download and experiment with the code, enhancing their hands-on learning experience.

Setting Up Your Development Environment

Choosing the Right Platform (iOS, Android, Cross-Platform Frameworks)

Selecting the right platform for mobile app development is one of the most critical decisions developers and businesses face. It influences the development tools, programming languages, user experience, and even the market reach of the application. Developers often choose between iOS, Android, or cross-platform frameworks based on various factors such as the target audience, app requirements, development resources, and project timeline.

1. iOS Development

iOS is Apple's mobile operating system, powering devices like the iPhone, iPad, and iPod Touch. Developing for iOS provides access to a high-value market, as Apple users tend to spend more on apps and services. However, iOS development comes with its own set of requirements and constraints.

Advantages of iOS Development:

- **User Base and Monetization Potential**: iOS users generally have higher purchasing power, which translates into better monetization opportunities through in-app purchases and premium app sales.

- **Performance Optimization**: Apple's closed ecosystem and tight integration between hardware and software (using Swift and Objective-C) allow for highly optimized and responsive applications.
- **Consistent Hardware and Software**: iOS developers benefit from a limited range of devices and OS versions, making it easier to ensure compatibility and maintain high-quality performance across devices.
- **Strong Ecosystem and Tools**: iOS development leverages tools like Xcode and technologies such as SwiftUI and UIKit, providing a robust environment for building efficient and visually appealing applications.

Challenges of iOS Development:

- **Restricted Platform**: iOS is exclusive to Apple hardware, limiting its reach to users within the Apple ecosystem. Developers targeting broader audiences may find this restrictive.
- **App Store Approval Process**: Apple's stringent app review process can be time-consuming and requires developers to adhere to strict guidelines to get their apps approved and listed in the App Store.
- **Licensing and Costs**: An Apple Developer Program subscription is required to publish apps on the App Store, and Mac hardware is necessary for development.

When to Choose iOS Development:

- When your target audience predominantly uses Apple devices.
- If you aim for high revenue generation through in-app purchases and subscriptions.
- If you prefer a controlled and optimized ecosystem with high security standards.

2. Android Development

Android, developed by Google, is the world's most popular mobile operating system, used by millions of devices worldwide. It powers a wide variety of smartphones and tablets from different manufacturers. Developing for Android offers access to a vast and diverse user base, but it also comes with challenges due to the fragmentation of hardware and software versions.

Advantages of Android Development:

- **Large Market Share**: Android holds the majority of the global market share, making it an attractive platform for developers targeting a broad and diverse audience.
- **Flexibility and Customization**: Android's open-source nature allows for greater flexibility and customization, enabling developers to build unique features and integrate with a wide range of hardware components.
- **Distribution Freedom**: Unlike iOS, Android developers can distribute their apps through multiple platforms, including the Google Play Store, Amazon Appstore, and even as APK files directly on websites.
- **Diverse Hardware Support**: Android supports a broad range of devices, from entry-level phones to high-end flagships, allowing developers to target different market segments.

Challenges of Android Development:

- **Fragmentation**: Android's diversity, while advantageous, leads to fragmentation issues. Developers must account for a wide array of screen sizes, hardware capabilities, and OS versions, making testing and optimization more complex.
- **Performance Variability**: Since Android devices range from low-end to high-end hardware, developers must ensure their apps perform well across all these devices, which may require additional optimization and testing.
- **Security Concerns**: Android's open nature and the ability to sideload apps increase the risk of security vulnerabilities. Developers need to implement robust security measures to protect their apps and users' data.

When to Choose Android Development:

- When your goal is to reach the largest possible audience, especially in emerging markets where Android devices are prevalent.
- If you want flexibility in app distribution beyond a single store (e.g., Google Play).
- When your application needs extensive hardware integration or customization that requires more control over the system.

3. Cross-Platform Development Frameworks

Cross-platform development frameworks, such as Flutter, React Native, and Xamarin, allow developers to write code once and deploy it across multiple platforms (iOS, Android, and sometimes web). These frameworks aim to reduce development time and cost by sharing codebases and minimizing the need for platform-specific coding.

Popular Cross-Platform Frameworks:

- **Flutter**: Developed by Google, Flutter uses the Dart programming language and allows for building natively compiled applications for mobile, web, and desktop from a single codebase. Its widget-based approach provides flexibility in UI design.
- **React Native**: Backed by Meta (formerly Facebook), React Native uses JavaScript and React to create cross-platform mobile applications. It provides near-native performance and a strong ecosystem of libraries and tools.
- **Xamarin**: Part of Microsoft's development suite, Xamarin uses C# and .NET to build cross-platform apps. It offers tight integration with Visual Studio, making it a suitable choice for developers already familiar with the Microsoft ecosystem.

Advantages of Cross-Platform Development:

- **Code Reusability**: Developers can write a single codebase that runs on multiple platforms, significantly reducing development time and maintenance efforts.

- **Cost-Effectiveness**: Cross-platform development is often more cost-effective, as it minimizes the need for separate development teams and resources for each platform.
- **Faster Time to Market**: With shared codebases, developers can simultaneously release apps on iOS and Android, accelerating the time to market.
- **Unified UI/UX**: These frameworks provide consistent UI/UX components across platforms, ensuring a uniform look and feel for the app.

Challenges of Cross-Platform Development:

- **Performance Overhead**: While cross-platform frameworks aim to provide near-native performance, they may still introduce performance overhead compared to fully native apps, especially for resource-intensive features.
- **Limited Access to Platform-Specific Features**: Some advanced or platform-specific features may require native code integration (bridging), adding complexity to the development process.
- **Dependency on Framework Updates**: Developers must rely on the cross-platform framework's community or maintainers for updates, which may lag behind platform-specific changes (e.g., new OS versions or hardware).

When to Choose Cross-Platform Development:

- If you need to target both iOS and Android with a limited budget and development resources.
- When rapid prototyping or proof-of-concept development is required.
- If you want to maintain a unified codebase for faster updates and easier maintenance.

Installing and Configuring Development Tools (Xcode, Android Studio, VS Code)

The development environment is an integral part of the mobile app development process, and configuring the right tools for the platform is crucial. Here's how to set up the most commonly used tools: Xcode (iOS), Android Studio (Android), and Visual Studio Code (cross-platform development).

1. Xcode (iOS Development)

Xcode is Apple's integrated development environment (IDE) for iOS, macOS, watchOS, and tvOS development. It is the primary tool for building iOS apps and offers a suite of features including code editing, debugging, UI design, and performance analysis.

Steps to Install and Configure Xcode:

- **System Requirements**: Xcode requires macOS. Ensure your Mac is running a compatible version of macOS (e.g., macOS Big Sur or later for the latest Xcode versions).
- **Download Xcode**: You can download Xcode from the Mac App Store or the Apple Developer website. Make sure to download the latest stable version.
- **Install Xcode**: Follow the installation instructions provided during the download process. The installation may take some time, depending on your internet speed and system performance.
- **Configure Developer Account**: To build and run iOS apps on a physical device, you need to sign in with your Apple ID or a developer account. Navigate to Xcode Preferences > Accounts, and add your Apple ID.
- **Set Up a New Project**: Once Xcode is installed, create a new project by selecting "Create a new Xcode project" from the startup window. Choose the appropriate template (e.g., App) and select Swift as the programming language.
- **Simulator Setup**: Xcode includes a simulator for testing apps without physical devices. Choose the simulator device from the toolbar and run the app to test basic functionality.

Key Features of Xcode:

- **SwiftUI and Interface Builder**: Xcode provides tools for designing user interfaces using SwiftUI or the visual Interface Builder. Developers can create responsive and dynamic layouts directly within the IDE.
- **Debugging Tools**: The debugger in Xcode offers breakpoints, stack tracing, and performance analysis tools, such as Instruments, for profiling memory, CPU, and other metrics.
- **Testing Frameworks**: Xcode supports XCTest for writing unit tests, UI tests, and performance tests to ensure app quality.

2. Android Studio (Android Development)

Android Studio is the official IDE for Android development, offering comprehensive tools for coding, debugging, and testing Android apps. It supports Java, Kotlin, and C++ and is compatible with Windows, macOS, and Linux.

Steps to Install and Configure Android Studio:

- **System Requirements**: Ensure your computer meets the minimum system requirements for Android Studio (Windows, macOS, or Linux). Visit the official Android Studio website for detailed system requirements.
- **Download Android Studio**: Go to the official website and download the latest version. Choose the installer suitable for your operating system.
- **Install Android Studio**: Follow the installation wizard to complete the setup. The process includes downloading the Android SDK (Software Development Kit) and necessary tools.
- **Configure SDK and Virtual Devices**: Open the Android Studio SDK Manager to ensure all required SDK components are installed. Next, set up an Android Virtual Device (AVD) using the AVD Manager for testing your app without a physical device.
- **Create a New Project**: Launch Android Studio and select "Start a new Android Studio project." Choose the appropriate project template (e.g., Empty Activity) and set up your project using Kotlin or Java.

- **Connect a Physical Device**: To test on a physical device, enable Developer Options and USB Debugging on your Android phone. Connect the device via USB and allow debugging permissions when prompted.

Key Features of Android Studio:

- **Layout Editor**: The visual layout editor helps developers design user interfaces with drag-and-drop components, constraint layouts, and real-time preview on different devices.
- **Code Assistance**: Android Studio provides intelligent code completion, linting, and code refactoring tools for Kotlin and Java.
- **Build System**: The Gradle build system manages dependencies and builds configurations, supporting modular and efficient app development.

3. Visual Studio Code (Cross-Platform Development)

Visual Studio Code (VS Code) is a lightweight, extensible code editor commonly used for cross-platform development with frameworks like Flutter, React Native, and Xamarin.

Steps to Install and Configure Visual Studio Code:

- **Download and Install VS Code**: Download VS Code from the official website for your operating system (Windows, macOS, or Linux). Follow the installation steps provided.
- **Install Extensions**: For mobile development, you'll need extensions like Flutter, Dart, or React Native. Install these from the VS Code marketplace by navigating to the Extensions view (Ctrl+Shift+X) and searching for the relevant tools.
- **Set Up SDKs**: Install the necessary SDKs based on the framework you choose. For Flutter, download the SDK from the Flutter website and add it to your system's PATH. For React Native, ensure you have Node.js, npm, and React Native CLI installed.
- **Configure Emulators**: Set up emulators or simulators compatible with

the chosen framework. For Flutter, VS Code integrates with Android Studio's AVD or Xcode's simulators. For React Native, you can use iOS simulators (macOS) or Android emulators.

- **Create and Run a Project**: Use VS Code's integrated terminal to create and run projects. For Flutter, execute flutter create my_app and for React Native, use npx react-native init MyApp. Open the project folder in VS Code and start coding.

Key Features of VS Code:

- **Customizable Environment**: VS Code supports a wide range of extensions, themes, and settings, allowing developers to tailor the environment to their workflow.
- **Integrated Terminal**: The terminal allows developers to execute commands, run projects, and manage dependencies without leaving the editor.
- **Debugging Capabilities**: VS Code supports debugging with break-points, watch variables, and call stack monitoring, compatible with Flutter, React Native, and other frameworks.

Creating Your First Mobile App Project

Creating your first mobile app project is an exciting step that sets the foundation for your development journey. Whether you are targeting iOS, Android, or using a cross-platform framework, the process involves setting up a new project in your development environment, understanding the basic structure, and running the app on a simulator or physical device.

1. **iOS: Creating a Mobile App Project with Xcode**
   Step-by-Step Guide:

- **Open Xcode**: Launch Xcode and choose "Create a new Xcode project" from the welcome screen.
- **Select a Template**: Xcode provides several templates. For a basic mobile app, choose the "App" template under the iOS tab.
- **Configure Project Settings**: Enter the project details:
- **Product Name**: The name of your app.
- **Team**: Your development team (if you're part of an Apple Developer Program).
- **Organization Identifier**: A reverse domain-style identifier (e.g., com.yourname.app).
- **Language**: Choose Swift for the programming language.
- **User Interface**: Select SwiftUI or UIKit, depending on your preference.
- **Set Up Project Files**: Xcode automatically sets up the basic files and folders for your project:
- **AppDelegate.swift** (for app lifecycle management).
- **ViewController.swift** (for managing the main view).
- **Main.storyboard** or **ContentView.swift** (for the UI layout, depending on your choice of SwiftUI or UIKit).
- **Run the App**: Choose a simulator from the device options and click the play button to build and run your app. If everything is set up correctly, you'll see a basic screen with your app's name.

Understanding the iOS Project Structure:

- **Info.plist**: Contains configuration settings for your app, such as permissions (camera access, network access), display name, and more.
- **AppDelegate.swift**: Manages the app lifecycle events such as launch, background state, and termination.
- **View Controllers**: These manage the content of the app's interface and respond to user interactions.

2. **Android: Creating a Mobile App Project with Android Studio Step-by-Step Guide:**

- **Open Android Studio**: Start Android Studio and click on "Start a new Android Studio project."
- **Choose a Project Template**: For a basic app, select "Empty Activity" to start with minimal setup. Other templates include login activity, master-detail flow, etc.
- **Configure Your Project**: Fill in the details:
- **Name**: The name of your application.
- **Package Name**: A unique identifier for your app (e.g., com.example.myapp).
- **Save Location**: Where your project files will be stored.
- **Language**: Choose between Kotlin and Java.
- **Minimum SDK**: Set the lowest version of Android your app will support. A lower number increases device compatibility but may limit available features.
- **Finish and Create Project**: Android Studio sets up your project files automatically. The main files include:
- **MainActivity.kt** (or **MainActivity.java**): The main entry point for your app, where you write code to manage the user interface and app behavior.
- **activity_main.xml**: The layout file for your main activity, which defines the UI components and layout structure.
- **Run the App**: Connect an Android emulator or physical device. Click the run button (green triangle) to build and launch your app on the device.

Understanding the Android Project Structure:

- **Manifest File** (AndroidManifest.xml): Contains essential app information such as permissions, activities, services, and the minimum SDK level.
- **Java/Kotlin Files**: Contain the code that defines the behavior of activities, fragments, and services.
- **Resource Folder** (res): Holds drawable resources (images), layout files (layout folder), and UI text (values folder).

3. Cross-Platform Frameworks: Creating a Mobile App Project (Flutter, React Native)

Using Flutter with VS Code:

- **Install Flutter**: Make sure Flutter SDK is installed and added to your PATH. Open VS Code and install the Flutter and Dart extensions.
- **Create a New Flutter Project**: Open VS Code's terminal and run flutter create myapp. This command sets up a basic project structure.
- **Explore the Project Files**: Flutter projects contain:
- **main.dart**: The main entry point of your app where you define the app structure using widgets.
- **pubspec.yaml**: A configuration file for managing dependencies, assets, and packages.
- **Run the App**: Connect a device or launch an emulator, then run flutter run in the terminal. The app should display a basic interface with a "Hello World" message.

Using React Native with VS Code:

- **Set Up React Native**: Ensure Node.js and npm are installed. Use the terminal to install the React Native CLI with npm install -g react-native-cli.
- **Create a New Project**: Run npx react-native init MyApp to generate a new project.
- **Explore the Project Files**: React Native projects contain:
- **App.js**: The main file where you define the UI and logic.
- **index.js**: The entry point that registers the app component.
- **Run the App**: Use npx react-native run-android or npx react-native run-ios to build and run the app on a connected emulator or device.

Understanding App Lifecycle and Concurrency Basics

Mobile app development requires understanding the app lifecycle, which involves the different states an app goes through from launch to termination. This knowledge is crucial, especially when implementing concurrency, to manage tasks efficiently and ensure a smooth user experience.

1. App Lifecycle in iOS

The iOS app lifecycle is managed primarily through the AppDelegate and SceneDelegate classes. Understanding these lifecycle stages helps developers manage app state transitions and implement concurrency effectively.

Key Lifecycle States:

- **Not Running**: The app is not launched or has been terminated.
- **Inactive**: The app is running but not receiving user input, such as when the user receives a call or switches to the app switcher.
- **Active**: The app is in the foreground and receiving events. This is the state where most user interactions occur.
- **Background**: The app is running but not visible to the user. This state allows for limited tasks like fetching data or processing tasks.
- **Suspended**: The app is in the background but not executing code. It remains in memory until the system needs resources.

Concurrency in iOS:

- **Grand Central Dispatch (GCD)**: GCD is a powerful API for managing concurrent code execution. It provides queues for executing tasks in the background or foreground:
- **Main Queue**: Handles tasks related to UI updates and runs on the main thread. UI updates should always occur on this queue to avoid UI freezing.
- **Global Queues**: Background queues for tasks like networking or data processing. These queues run tasks concurrently, allowing the app to remain responsive.

- **Operation Queues**: These provide more control over task execution, including dependencies, priorities, and canceling tasks. Developers use operation queues when they need more complex task management beyond GCD's capabilities.

Example: Fetching Data Using Concurrency in iOS

- When making a network request to fetch data, developers use a background queue to handle the task:

```swift
Copy code
DispatchQueue.global(qos: .background).async {
    // Perform network request
    let data = fetchDataFromServer()
    DispatchQueue.main.async {
        // Update the UI with the fetched data
        updateUI(with: data)
    }
}
```

- This approach ensures the UI remains responsive while the network operation runs in the background.

2. App Lifecycle in Android

The Android app lifecycle is primarily managed through activities, each representing a single screen of an app. Understanding these lifecycle events allows developers to manage resources efficiently and implement concurrency effectively.

Key Lifecycle Methods:

- **onCreate()**: Called when the activity is first created. This is where initialization logic, like setting up the UI and variables, occurs.

- **onStart()**: Called when the activity becomes visible to the user.
- **onResume()**: Called when the activity starts interacting with the user. It's where most of the app's core functionality occurs.
- **onPause()**: Called when the activity is partially obscured (e.g., another activity is placed on top of it). Developers often use this method to pause ongoing tasks.
- **onStop()**: Called when the activity is no longer visible. Resources can be released here to improve app performance.
- **onDestroy()**: Called before the activity is destroyed. It's the final opportunity to clean up resources.

Concurrency in Android:

- **Threads**: The simplest way to run tasks concurrently in Android is by creating new threads. However, managing them directly can be error-prone and inefficient for complex tasks.
- **AsyncTask (Deprecated)**: Used to manage background operations with methods for pre- and post-execution. Although it's deprecated, it introduced developers to the basics of handling background tasks.
- **Kotlin Coroutines**: The modern approach in Android for concurrency. Coroutines simplify asynchronous programming by allowing developers to write code sequentially while still being asynchronous:

```kotlin
Copy code
GlobalScope.launch {
    val data = fetchDataFromNetwork()
    withContext(Dispatchers.Main) {
        updateUI(data)
    }
}
```

- **WorkManager**: A solution for managing background tasks that need to be guaranteed to run, even after app restarts. It's useful for tasks like data synchronization or uploading logs.

3. Cross-Platform App Lifecycle and Concurrency Basics

Cross-platform frameworks abstract the platform-specific details while providing developers with similar lifecycle management capabilities:

Flutter App Lifecycle:

- **Widgets and State**: Flutter apps revolve around widgets and their state. The lifecycle of a widget is managed using hooks like initState(), build(), and dispose().
- **Concurrency**: Flutter uses Dart's Future and async/await for concurrency, making it easy to handle asynchronous code:

```dart
Copy code
Future<void> fetchData() async {
  final data = await fetchDataFromApi();
  setState(() {
    _data = data;
  });
}
```

- Flutter's Isolates enable true parallel execution, though they are more complex to manage than Dart's async/await.

React Native App Lifecycle:

- **Component Lifecycle Methods**: React Native uses component lifecycle methods like componentDidMount and componentWillUnmount to manage app states.
- **Concurrency**: JavaScript's async/await is commonly used to handle asynchronous tasks. Native modules also provide concurrency support

for tasks that require more intensive computation or background processing.

Understanding Concurrency: Concepts and Principles

What is Concurrency?

C oncurrency is the ability of a program to manage multiple tasks at the same time, allowing for the efficient use of system resources like CPU and memory. In mobile app development, concurrency is essential for creating responsive and efficient applications that can handle tasks such as user interactions, network requests, and background processing without causing delays or freezing the user interface (UI).

At its core, concurrency involves dividing tasks into smaller, manageable units that can be executed independently or in parallel. This means that instead of waiting for one task to complete before starting another, tasks can run simultaneously or be interleaved, allowing the program to utilize resources more effectively and improve performance.

Concurrency is not limited to executing tasks simultaneously (parallelism) but also involves structuring tasks to work cooperatively. In a mobile app, for example, concurrency might involve handling user input, processing network requests, and updating the UI—all seemingly at once, even if the underlying operations are managed in a way that they take turns using the processor.

Benefits of Concurrency in Mobile Development:

1. **Improved Responsiveness**: Concurrency allows the app to remain responsive to user interactions even when performing long-running tasks, such as downloading data from a server or processing images.
2. **Efficient Resource Utilization**: By distributing tasks across different threads or cores, concurrency optimizes the use of system resources, leading to better performance and energy efficiency, which is crucial for battery-powered mobile devices.
3. **Scalability**: Concurrency enables the app to handle multiple tasks at once, making it easier to scale up as the app becomes more complex, such as handling more user requests or integrating advanced features like real-time data processing.

Concurrency, however, also introduces complexity. Managing multiple tasks requires careful synchronization and coordination to avoid issues like race conditions (where two tasks try to access the same resource simultaneously) or deadlocks (where tasks wait on each other indefinitely). Developers use various concurrency models and tools, such as multithreading, event loops, and asynchronous programming, to implement concurrency effectively.

Synchronous vs. Asynchronous Programming

A key concept in concurrency is the distinction between synchronous and asynchronous programming. Understanding these two approaches is fundamental to implementing effective concurrency in mobile apps.

Synchronous Programming

In synchronous programming, tasks are executed sequentially. One task must complete before the next task begins. This linear approach is simple to understand and easy to implement but can lead to inefficiencies and a poor user experience, especially in mobile apps where responsiveness is crucial.

Example: Imagine an app that fetches data from an API and then displays the results to the user. In a synchronous approach, the app would:

1. Start the network request.

28

2. Wait for the response.
3. Process the data.
4. Update the UI.

During the time it takes to fetch the data (which may take several seconds), the app is blocked—no other operations can occur. The user cannot interact with the app, leading to a frozen or unresponsive experience.

Pros of Synchronous Programming:

- Simple to implement and understand.
- Predictable flow of control, making it easier to debug.

Cons of Synchronous Programming:

- Poor user experience for time-consuming tasks (e.g., network requests or file operations).
- Inefficient use of system resources, as the program remains idle while waiting for tasks to complete.

Asynchronous Programming

In contrast, asynchronous programming allows tasks to be executed without blocking the flow of the program. When an asynchronous task is initiated, the program continues to execute other code while waiting for the task to complete. Once the task finishes, a callback function or event handler processes the result.

Example: Consider the same app that fetches data from an API. In an asynchronous approach:

1. The network request is initiated.
2. The app continues executing other code (e.g., allowing the user to navigate or interact with the UI).
3. When the network request completes, a callback function is executed to process the data and update the UI.

This approach ensures that the app remains responsive and can handle multiple operations concurrently.

Pros of Asynchronous Programming:

- Keeps the app responsive, providing a smoother user experience.
- Optimizes the use of resources by allowing other tasks to run while waiting for long-running operations.

Cons of Asynchronous Programming:

- More complex to implement and understand, as it involves managing callbacks, event handlers, or promises.
- Can lead to bugs if tasks are not synchronized properly, especially when accessing shared resources.

Asynchronous Patterns and Tools

Asynchronous programming is implemented differently across programming languages and platforms. Here are some common patterns and tools used in mobile app development:

1. **Callbacks**:

- A function is passed as an argument to be called once the task is complete. While simple, it can lead to "callback hell" if multiple levels of callbacks are nested.

1. **Promises (JavaScript)**:

- Promises provide a cleaner way to handle asynchronous code by chaining operations, making the flow easier to read and manage.

1. **Async/Await (Swift, Kotlin, JavaScript)**:

- Modern languages like Swift, Kotlin, and JavaScript support async/await syntax, which allows developers to write asynchronous code in a synchronous style. It makes code more readable and easier to manage while retaining the benefits of asynchronous execution.

1. **Coroutines (Kotlin):**

- Kotlin's coroutines provide a powerful way to handle asynchronous tasks, allowing developers to suspend and resume functions without blocking threads. This simplifies managing complex operations like network requests, database access, or parallel processing.

Multithreading: Core Concepts and Use Cases

Multithreading is a concurrency model where multiple threads of execution run simultaneously within a program. Each thread can be thought of as a separate path of execution, allowing tasks to run in parallel or be interleaved efficiently. In mobile app development, multithreading is crucial for handling background operations, ensuring apps remain responsive while performing complex tasks like data processing or network communication.

Core Concepts of Multithreading

1. **Thread:**

- A thread is the smallest unit of execution within a process. Each app runs in its process, and within that process, multiple threads can execute concurrently. The main thread, also called the UI thread, is responsible for handling user input and updating the interface. Developers create additional threads for background tasks to keep the main thread free for UI operations.

1. **Main Thread (UI Thread):**

- In mobile apps, the main thread is crucial as it handles all UI updates and user interactions. Blocking the main thread with long-running tasks, such as network requests or heavy computations, results in an unresponsive app. Therefore, developers must offload these tasks to background threads to maintain a smooth user experience.

1. **Background Threads**:

- Background threads are used for tasks that do not require immediate interaction with the user, such as downloading data, parsing files, or performing computations. These threads operate independently of the main thread, ensuring that the app remains responsive.
- Developers use various APIs to manage background threads, such as Thread in Java, DispatchQueue in Swift, and coroutines in Kotlin.

1. **Thread Pool**:

- A thread pool is a collection of pre-instantiated threads managed by a task scheduler. It optimizes the use of threads by reusing them for different tasks, reducing the overhead associated with creating and destroying threads.
- Thread pools are particularly useful for executing a large number of short-lived tasks efficiently, such as handling network requests or processing small chunks of data concurrently.

Use Cases of Multithreading in Mobile App Development

1. **Network Operations**:

- Fetching data from APIs, downloading files, or uploading media requires time and can block the main thread if not handled properly. Developers use background threads to manage these network operations, ensuring that the app remains responsive while data is being fetched or uploaded.

- In Android, developers might use Kotlin coroutines or the OkHttp library with enqueue for asynchronous network calls. In iOS, developers can use URLSession with DispatchQueue for similar purposes.

1. **Data Processing and File Operations**:

- Mobile apps often need to read, write, or process large amounts of data, such as parsing JSON, reading files, or compressing images. Performing these operations on the main thread can cause the app to freeze. Background threads are used to handle these tasks efficiently.
- For example, in an image-editing app, applying filters or resizing images can be offloaded to a background thread while keeping the main thread available for user interaction.

1. **UI Updates and Animations**:

- While most UI updates must occur on the main thread, background threads can prepare the necessary data before passing it to the main thread for rendering. For example, in a messaging app, incoming messages can be processed and formatted in the background, while the UI thread updates the chat view.
- Animations must also be managed carefully to avoid blocking the main thread. Some platforms provide APIs for running animations on separate threads or using dedicated animation frameworks.

1. **Database Operations**:

- Accessing and modifying data stored in a local database (e.g., SQLite, Core Data) can be time-consuming. Performing database operations on the main thread can lead to a sluggish UI, especially when dealing with large datasets or complex queries.
- In Android, developers often use libraries like Room with coroutines to perform asynchronous database operations. In iOS, Core Data provides

33

mechanisms to manage background contexts, allowing data to be fetched and processed without blocking the UI.

1. **Multimedia Processing**:

- Apps that handle video editing, real-time image filtering, or audio processing need to manage these tasks on background threads. Multimedia processing is resource-intensive and can significantly impact performance if not handled concurrently.
- In iOS, developers can use frameworks like AVFoundation and Core Image with multithreading to perform these tasks efficiently. In Android, libraries like MediaCodec and CameraX support multithreaded processing for video and camera apps.

Challenges of Multithreading

While multithreading is powerful, it also introduces complexity. Developers must handle the following challenges:

1. **Race Conditions**:

- Occur when multiple threads access shared data concurrently without proper synchronization, leading to inconsistent results. Developers use locks, mutexes, or synchronized methods to prevent race conditions, but these can introduce performance bottlenecks if overused.

1. **Deadlocks**:

- Arise when two or more threads wait indefinitely for each other to release resources. Properly structuring code and avoiding circular dependencies between threads are essential to prevent deadlocks.

1. **Thread Synchronization**:

- Coordinating the execution of threads is crucial when they share resources or need to communicate results. Developers use semaphores, barriers, and other synchronization mechanisms to manage thread interactions.

1. **Debugging Multithreaded Applications**:

- Debugging issues in multithreaded apps can be challenging because errors may only appear under specific conditions or workloads. Debugging tools like Instruments (iOS) and the Android Profiler help track thread activity and diagnose concurrency issues.

What is Concurrency?

Concurrency is the ability of a program to manage multiple tasks at the same time, allowing for the efficient use of system resources like CPU and memory. In mobile app development, concurrency is essential for creating responsive and efficient applications that can handle tasks such as user interactions, network requests, and background processing without causing delays or freezing the user interface (UI).

At its core, concurrency involves dividing tasks into smaller, manageable units that can be executed independently or in parallel. This means that instead of waiting for one task to complete before starting another, tasks can run simultaneously or be interleaved, allowing the program to utilize resources more effectively and improve performance.

Concurrency is not limited to executing tasks simultaneously (parallelism) but also involves structuring tasks to work cooperatively. In a mobile app, for example, concurrency might involve handling user input, processing network requests, and updating the UI—all seemingly at once, even if the underlying operations are managed in a way that they take turns using the processor.

Benefits of Concurrency in Mobile Development:

1. **Improved Responsiveness**: Concurrency allows the app to remain responsive to user interactions even when performing long-running tasks, such as downloading data from a server or processing images.
2. **Efficient Resource Utilization**: By distributing tasks across different threads or cores, concurrency optimizes the use of system resources, leading to better performance and energy efficiency, which is crucial for battery-powered mobile devices.
3. **Scalability**: Concurrency enables the app to handle multiple tasks at once, making it easier to scale up as the app becomes more complex, such as handling more user requests or integrating advanced features like real-time data processing.

Concurrency, however, also introduces complexity. Managing multiple tasks requires careful synchronization and coordination to avoid issues like race conditions (where two tasks try to access the same resource simultaneously) or deadlocks (where tasks wait on each other indefinitely). Developers use various concurrency models and tools, such as multithreading, event loops, and asynchronous programming, to implement concurrency effectively.

Synchronous vs. Asynchronous Programming

A key concept in concurrency is the distinction between synchronous and asynchronous programming. Understanding these two approaches is fundamental to implementing effective concurrency in mobile apps.

Synchronous Programming

In synchronous programming, tasks are executed sequentially. One task must complete before the next task begins. This linear approach is simple to understand and easy to implement but can lead to inefficiencies and a poor user experience, especially in mobile apps where responsiveness is crucial.

Example: Imagine an app that fetches data from an API and then displays the results to the user. In a synchronous approach, the app would:

1. Start the network request.

2. Wait for the response.
3. Process the data.
4. Update the UI.

During the time it takes to fetch the data (which may take several seconds), the app is blocked—no other operations can occur. The user cannot interact with the app, leading to a frozen or unresponsive experience.

Pros of Synchronous Programming:

- Simple to implement and understand.
- Predictable flow of control, making it easier to debug.

Cons of Synchronous Programming:

- Poor user experience for time-consuming tasks (e.g., network requests or file operations).
- Inefficient use of system resources, as the program remains idle while waiting for tasks to complete.

Asynchronous Programming

In contrast, asynchronous programming allows tasks to be executed without blocking the flow of the program. When an asynchronous task is initiated, the program continues to execute other code while waiting for the task to complete. Once the task finishes, a callback function or event handler processes the result.

Example: Consider the same app that fetches data from an API. In an asynchronous approach:

1. The network request is initiated.
2. The app continues executing other code (e.g., allowing the user to navigate or interact with the UI).
3. When the network request completes, a callback function is executed to process the data and update the UI.

This approach ensures that the app remains responsive and can handle multiple operations concurrently.

Pros of Asynchronous Programming:

- Keeps the app responsive, providing a smoother user experience.
- Optimizes the use of resources by allowing other tasks to run while waiting for long-running operations.

Cons of Asynchronous Programming:

- More complex to implement and understand, as it involves managing callbacks, event handlers, or promises.
- Can lead to bugs if tasks are not synchronized properly, especially when accessing shared resources.

Asynchronous Patterns and Tools

Asynchronous programming is implemented differently across programming languages and platforms. Here are some common patterns and tools used in mobile app development:

1. **Callbacks**:

- A function is passed as an argument to be called once the task is complete. While simple, it can lead to "callback hell" if multiple levels of callbacks are nested.

1. **Promises (JavaScript)**:

- Promises provide a cleaner way to handle asynchronous code by chaining operations, making the flow easier to read and manage.

1. **Async/Await (Swift, Kotlin, JavaScript)**:

- Modern languages like Swift, Kotlin, and JavaScript support async/await syntax, which allows developers to write asynchronous code in a synchronous style. It makes code more readable and easier to manage while retaining the benefits of asynchronous execution.

1. **Coroutines (Kotlin)**:

- Kotlin's coroutines provide a powerful way to handle asynchronous tasks, allowing developers to suspend and resume functions without blocking threads. This simplifies managing complex operations like network requests, database access, or parallel processing.

Multithreading: Core Concepts and Use Cases

Multithreading is a concurrency model where multiple threads of execution run simultaneously within a program. Each thread can be thought of as a separate path of execution, allowing tasks to run in parallel or be interleaved efficiently. In mobile app development, multithreading is crucial for handling background operations, ensuring apps remain responsive while performing complex tasks like data processing or network communication.

Core Concepts of Multithreading

1. **Thread**:

- A thread is the smallest unit of execution within a process. Each app runs in its process, and within that process, multiple threads can execute concurrently. The main thread, also called the UI thread, is responsible for handling user input and updating the interface. Developers create additional threads for background tasks to keep the main thread free for UI operations.

1. **Main Thread (UI Thread)**:

- In mobile apps, the main thread is crucial as it handles all UI updates and user interactions. Blocking the main thread with long-running tasks, such as network requests or heavy computations, results in an unresponsive app. Therefore, developers must offload these tasks to background threads to maintain a smooth user experience.

1. **Background Threads**:

- Background threads are used for tasks that do not require immediate interaction with the user, such as downloading data, parsing files, or performing computations. These threads operate independently of the main thread, ensuring that the app remains responsive.
- Developers use various APIs to manage background threads, such as Thread in Java, DispatchQueue in Swift, and coroutines in Kotlin.

1. **Thread Pool**:

- A thread pool is a collection of pre-instantiated threads managed by a task scheduler. It optimizes the use of threads by reusing them for different tasks, reducing the overhead associated with creating and destroying threads.
- Thread pools are particularly useful for executing a large number of short-lived tasks efficiently, such as handling network requests or processing small chunks of data concurrently.

Use Cases of Multithreading in Mobile App Development

1. **Network Operations**:

- Fetching data from APIs, downloading files, or uploading media requires time and can block the main thread if not handled properly. Developers use background threads to manage these network operations, ensuring that the app remains responsive while data is being fetched or uploaded.

- In Android, developers might use Kotlin coroutines or the OkHttp library with enqueue for asynchronous network calls. In iOS, developers can use URLSession with DispatchQueue for similar purposes.

1. **Data Processing and File Operations**:

- Mobile apps often need to read, write, or process large amounts of data, such as parsing JSON, reading files, or compressing images. Performing these operations on the main thread can cause the app to freeze. Background threads are used to handle these tasks efficiently.
- For example, in an image-editing app, applying filters or resizing images can be offloaded to a background thread while keeping the main thread available for user interaction.

1. **UI Updates and Animations**:

- While most UI updates must occur on the main thread, background threads can prepare the necessary data before passing it to the main thread for rendering. For example, in a messaging app, incoming messages can be processed and formatted in the background, while the UI thread updates the chat view.
- Animations must also be managed carefully to avoid blocking the main thread. Some platforms provide APIs for running animations on separate threads or using dedicated animation frameworks.

1. **Database Operations**:

- Accessing and modifying data stored in a local database (e.g., SQLite, Core Data) can be time-consuming. Performing database operations on the main thread can lead to a sluggish UI, especially when dealing with large datasets or complex queries.
- In Android, developers often use libraries like Room with coroutines to perform asynchronous database operations. In iOS, Core Data provides

41

mechanisms to manage background contexts, allowing data to be fetched and processed without blocking the UI.

1. **Multimedia Processing**:

- Apps that handle video editing, real-time image filtering, or audio processing need to manage these tasks on background threads. Multimedia processing is resource-intensive and can significantly impact performance if not handled concurrently.
- In iOS, developers can use frameworks like AVFoundation and Core Image with multithreading to perform these tasks efficiently. In Android, libraries like MediaCodec and CameraX support multithreaded processing for video and camera apps.

Challenges of Multithreading

While multithreading is powerful, it also introduces complexity. Developers must handle the following challenges:

1. **Race Conditions**:

- Occur when multiple threads access shared data concurrently without proper synchronization, leading to inconsistent results. Developers use locks, mutexes, or synchronized methods to prevent race conditions, but these can introduce performance bottlenecks if overused.

1. **Deadlocks**:

- Arise when two or more threads wait indefinitely for each other to release resources. Properly structuring code and avoiding circular dependencies between threads are essential to prevent deadlocks.

1. **Thread Synchronization**:

- Coordinating the execution of threads is crucial when they share resources or need to communicate results. Developers use semaphores, barriers, and other synchronization mechanisms to manage thread interactions.

1. **Debugging Multithreaded Applications**:

- Debugging issues in multithreaded apps can be challenging because errors may only appear under specific conditions or workloads. Debugging tools like Instruments (iOS) and the Android Profiler help track thread activity and diagnose concurrency issues.

Summary

Concurrency, and specifically multithreading, is a fundamental aspect of mobile app development. It enables apps to manage multiple tasks efficiently, providing responsive and scalable experiences for users. Understanding the differences between synchronous and asynchronous programming, as well as the core concepts and use cases of multithreading, equips developers with the tools they need to build high-performance mobile applications. By managing threads and tasks effectively, developers can harness the power of concurrency while avoiding common pitfalls, ensuring that their apps run smoothly and efficiently.

4o
You said:
Task-Based Concurrency and Event-Driven Programming Common Challenges in Concurrency (Deadlocks, Race Conditions)

ChatGPT said:
ChatGPT

Task-Based Concurrency and Event-Driven Programming

Task-based concurrency and event-driven programming are fundamental approaches for implementing concurrency in mobile app development. These models help developers manage multiple tasks and events efficiently, ensuring applications remain responsive and efficient.

Task-Based Concurrency

Task-based concurrency is a concurrency model that focuses on organizing work into tasks, which are units of work that can be executed independently. Unlike thread-based models where developers directly manage threads, task-based concurrency abstracts the complexity by using higher-level constructs like tasks, queues, or promises. This approach makes it easier to write and manage concurrent code.

Key Concepts in Task-Based Concurrency

1. **Tasks**:

- A task is an independent unit of work that can be executed asynchronously. It may involve any operation, such as fetching data from an API, processing an image, or performing a calculation.
- Tasks are often created, executed, and managed by a task scheduler or a task queue, which handles the scheduling and execution of tasks based on system resources and priorities.

1. **Task Queues**:

- Task queues organize and manage the execution of tasks. Developers add tasks to these queues, which are processed concurrently or sequentially, depending on the configuration.
- **Examples**: Grand Central Dispatch (GCD) in iOS uses queues (DispatchQueue) to manage tasks. Similarly, in Android, the Executor framework provides a mechanism for managing task execution using thread pools.

1. Task Scheduling:

- In task-based concurrency, tasks are scheduled based on availability of system resources, priority levels, or dependencies. For instance, some tasks might need to wait for others to complete before they can execute.
- **Task-Based Libraries**: Libraries like Swift's Combine framework, Kotlin's coroutines, and Java's CompletableFuture simplify task scheduling and management.

1. Benefits of Task-Based Concurrency:

- **Abstraction**: Developers can focus on defining tasks rather than managing low-level thread behavior, making the code more readable and maintainable.
- **Scalability**: Task-based models can scale better as they allow dynamic adjustment based on system resources and workload.
- **Error Handling**: Task-based frameworks often provide built-in mechanisms for managing errors, retries, and task cancellation.

Example: Using Task-Based Concurrency in Mobile Apps
iOS (Swift with GCD):

```swift
Copy code
DispatchQueue.global(qos: .userInitiated).async {
    // Background task: fetching data from server
    let data = fetchDataFromServer()
    DispatchQueue.main.async {
        // Update UI with the fetched data
        updateUI(data: data)
    }
}
```

- In this example, a task is added to a background queue for fetching data asynchronously. Once the data is fetched, another task on the main queue updates the UI, ensuring the app remains responsive.

Android (Kotlin Coroutines):

```kotlin
Copy code
GlobalScope.launch {
    val result = fetchDataFromApi() // Background task
    withContext(Dispatchers.Main) {
        updateUI(result) // UI update on the main thread
    }
}
```

- Kotlin coroutines make it easy to write asynchronous code in a sequential style. The background operation runs in a coroutine, and the result is handled on the main thread.

Event-Driven Programming

Event-driven programming is a programming paradigm where the flow of the program is determined by events. These events can be user interactions (e.g., button clicks), system-generated events (e.g., network availability changes), or other triggers (e.g., timer completions). In mobile app development, event-driven programming is essential for creating interactive and responsive applications.

Key Concepts in Event-Driven Programming

1. **Events**:

- Events are actions or occurrences that the system recognizes and responds to. Examples include user interactions like taps or swipes, sensor readings, or changes in network status.

1. **Event Handlers**:

- Event handlers are functions or methods that respond to specific events. They are registered to listen for certain events and execute code when those events occur. For instance, in a button click event handler, code to process the click action is executed when the button is tapped.

1. **Event Loops**:

- An event loop is a core mechanism in event-driven programming that continuously checks for new events and dispatches them to appropriate event handlers. The event loop ensures that events are processed asynchronously, allowing the main thread to remain responsive.
- **Examples**: In JavaScript (React Native), the event loop manages user events and system events. Similarly, in iOS and Android, the frameworks handle event loops behind the scenes to manage user interactions and system notifications.

1. **Frameworks Supporting Event-Driven Programming**:

- Many mobile app development frameworks (e.g., Flutter, React Native) are inherently event-driven, allowing developers to define components and attach event handlers to manage user interactions.

Example: Event-Driven Programming in Mobile Apps
iOS (Swift):

```swift
Copy code
@IBAction func buttonTapped(_ sender: UIButton) {
    // Code to handle the button tap event
    performAction()
}
```

- This example shows an event handler (buttonTapped) that responds when

47

a button is tapped, executing a function to perform an action.

Android (Kotlin):

```kotlin
kotlin
Copy code
button.setOnClickListener {
    // Code to handle the button click event
    performAction()
}
```

- In Android, event listeners like setOnClickListener respond to user actions such as button clicks.

Common Challenges in Concurrency

Concurrency, while powerful, introduces complexity into software development. It requires careful management to avoid issues like deadlocks and race conditions, which can cause unpredictable behavior, crashes, or performance problems.

1. Deadlocks

A deadlock occurs when two or more threads are blocked indefinitely, waiting for each other to release resources. This situation can arise when multiple threads hold locks and each thread waits for a lock held by another thread. Since no thread can proceed, the program stalls.

Example of a Deadlock

Imagine two threads (Thread A and Thread B) and two resources (Resource 1 and Resource 2):

1. Thread A locks Resource 1 and waits for Resource 2 to be released.
2. Thread B locks Resource 2 and waits for Resource 1 to be released.

Since both threads are waiting for resources held by the other, they are in a deadlock.

Avoiding Deadlocks

1. **Lock Ordering**:

- Enforce a consistent order for acquiring locks. If all threads acquire resources in the same order, deadlocks can be avoided because no circular dependency will form.

1. **Timeouts and Lock Timeouts**:

- Use timeouts when acquiring locks. If a thread cannot acquire a lock within a specified time, it can release other resources it holds, back off, and try again later. This prevents threads from being blocked indefinitely.

1. **Deadlock Detection**:

- Some programming environments provide tools to detect deadlocks. By analyzing the dependency graph of threads and resources, developers can identify potential deadlocks and adjust their code accordingly.

1. **Using Non-Blocking Algorithms**:

- Non-blocking algorithms, like using atomic operations (e.g., compare-and-swap), reduce the need for locks and minimize the risk of deadlocks.

2. Race Conditions

A race condition occurs when two or more threads access shared data simultaneously, and at least one of the threads modifies the data. If the threads' operations are not properly synchronized, this can lead to unpredictable or incorrect behavior.

Example of a Race Condition

Consider a counter variable accessed by multiple threads:

1. Thread A reads the value of the counter (e.g., 5).
2. Before Thread A updates the counter, Thread B also reads the counter value (still 5).
3. Both threads increment the counter and write the value back (6), instead of incrementing it twice (to 7).

In this scenario, the final value of the counter is incorrect because the two threads interfered with each other's operations.

Avoiding Race Conditions

1. **Synchronization Mechanisms**:

- Use synchronization primitives like mutexes, locks, or synchronized blocks (in Java/Kotlin) to ensure that only one thread accesses critical sections of code at a time. This prevents multiple threads from modifying shared data simultaneously.

1. **Atomic Operations**:

- Atomic operations are indivisible actions that guarantee the operation is completed fully before another thread can intervene. Programming languages often provide atomic classes (e.g., AtomicInteger in Java) to handle simple operations without needing full synchronization.

1. **Immutable Objects**:

- Immutable objects cannot be modified after creation. By using immutable objects, developers eliminate the risk of race conditions, as multiple threads can safely read the object without conflicts.

1. **Thread-Safe Data Structures**:

- Many programming languages offer thread-safe data structures (e.g.,

ConcurrentHashMap in Java) that manage synchronization internally, allowing multiple threads to access and modify data safely
- Task-Based Concurrency and Event-Driven Programming

Task-based concurrency and event-driven programming are fundamental approaches for implementing concurrency in mobile app development. These models help developers manage multiple tasks and events efficiently, ensuring applications remain responsive and efficient.

Task-Based Concurrency

Task-based concurrency is a concurrency model that focuses on organizing work into tasks, which are units of work that can be executed independently. Unlike thread-based models where developers directly manage threads, task-based concurrency abstracts the complexity by using higher-level constructs like tasks, queues, or promises. This approach makes it easier to write and manage concurrent code.

Key Concepts in Task-Based Concurrency

- **Tasks**:
- A task is an independent unit of work that can be executed asynchronously. It may involve any operation, such as fetching data from an API, processing an image, or performing a calculation.
- Tasks are often created, executed, and managed by a task scheduler or a task queue, which handles the scheduling and execution of tasks based on system resources and priorities.
- **Task Queues**:
- Task queues organize and manage the execution of tasks. Developers add tasks to these queues, which are processed concurrently or sequentially, depending on the configuration.
- **Examples**: Grand Central Dispatch (GCD) in iOS uses queues (DispatchQueue) to manage tasks. Similarly, in Android, the Executor framework provides a mechanism for managing task execution using thread pools.
- **Task Scheduling**:

- In task-based concurrency, tasks are scheduled based on availability of system resources, priority levels, or dependencies. For instance, some tasks might need to wait for others to complete before they can execute.
- **Task-Based Libraries**: Libraries like Swift's Combine framework, Kotlin's coroutines, and Java's CompletableFuture simplify task scheduling and management.
- **Benefits of Task-Based Concurrency**:
- **Abstraction**: Developers can focus on defining tasks rather than managing low-level thread behavior, making the code more readable and maintainable.
- **Scalability**: Task-based models can scale better as they allow dynamic adjustment based on system resources and workload.
- **Error Handling**: Task-based frameworks often provide built-in mechanisms for managing errors, retries, and task cancellation.

Example: Using Task-Based Concurrency in Mobile Apps
iOS (Swift with GCD):

- swift
- Copy code
- DispatchQueue.global(qos: .userInitiated).async {
- // Background task: fetching data from server
- let data = fetchDataFromServer()
- DispatchQueue.main.async {
- // Update UI with the fetched data
- updateUI(data: data)
- }
- }
- In this example, a task is added to a background queue for fetching data asynchronously. Once the data is fetched, another task on the main queue updates the UI, ensuring the app remains responsive.

Android (Kotlin Coroutines):

- kotlin
- Copy code
- GlobalScope.launch {
- val result = fetchDataFromApi() // Background task
- withContext(Dispatchers.Main) {
- updateUI(result) // UI update on the main thread
- }
- }
- Kotlin coroutines make it easy to write asynchronous code in a sequential style. The background operation runs in a coroutine, and the result is handled on the main thread.

Event-Driven Programming

Event-driven programming is a programming paradigm where the flow of the program is determined by events. These events can be user interactions (e.g., button clicks), system-generated events (e.g., network availability changes), or other triggers (e.g., timer completions). In mobile app development, event-driven programming is essential for creating interactive and responsive applications.

Key Concepts in Event-Driven Programming

- **Events**:
- Events are actions or occurrences that the system recognizes and responds to. Examples include user interactions like taps or swipes, sensor readings, or changes in network status.
- **Event Handlers**:
- Event handlers are functions or methods that respond to specific events. They are registered to listen for certain events and execute code when those events occur. For instance, in a button click event handler, code to process the click action is executed when the button is tapped.
- **Event Loops**:
- An event loop is a core mechanism in event-driven programming that continuously checks for new events and dispatches them to appropriate

event handlers. The event loop ensures that events are processed asynchronously, allowing the main thread to remain responsive.

- **Examples**: In JavaScript (React Native), the event loop manages user events and system events. Similarly, in iOS and Android, the frameworks handle event loops behind the scenes to manage user interactions and system notifications.
- **Frameworks Supporting Event-Driven Programming**:
- Many mobile app development frameworks (e.g., Flutter, React Native) are inherently event-driven, allowing developers to define components and attach event handlers to manage user interactions.

Example: Event-Driven Programming in Mobile Apps
iOS (Swift):

- swift
- Copy code
- @IBAction func buttonTapped(_ sender: UIButton) {
- // Code to handle the button tap event
- performAction()
- }
- This example shows an event handler (buttonTapped) that responds when a button is tapped, executing a function to perform an action.

Android (Kotlin):

- kotlin
- Copy code
- button.setOnClickListener {
- // Code to handle the button click event
- performAction()
- }
- In Android, event listeners like setOnClickListener respond to user actions such as button clicks.

- Common Challenges in Concurrency

Concurrency, while powerful, introduces complexity into software development. It requires careful management to avoid issues like deadlocks and race conditions, which can cause unpredictable behavior, crashes, or performance problems.

1. Deadlocks

A deadlock occurs when two or more threads are blocked indefinitely, waiting for each other to release resources. This situation can arise when multiple threads hold locks and each thread waits for a lock held by another thread. Since no thread can proceed, the program stalls.

Example of a Deadlock

Imagine two threads (Thread A and Thread B) and two resources (Resource 1 and Resource 2):

- Thread A locks Resource 1 and waits for Resource 2 to be released.
- Thread B locks Resource 2 and waits for Resource 1 to be released.

Since both threads are waiting for resources held by the other, they are in a deadlock.

Avoiding Deadlocks

- **Lock Ordering**:
- Enforce a consistent order for acquiring locks. If all threads acquire resources in the same order, deadlocks can be avoided because no circular dependency will form.
- **Timeouts and Lock Timeouts**:
- Use timeouts when acquiring locks. If a thread cannot acquire a lock within a specified time, it can release other resources it holds, back off, and try again later. This prevents threads from being blocked indefinitely.
- **Deadlock Detection**:
- Some programming environments provide tools to detect deadlocks. By analyzing the dependency graph of threads and resources, developers

can identify potential deadlocks and adjust their code accordingly.
- **Using Non-Blocking Algorithms**:
- Non-blocking algorithms, like using atomic operations (e.g., compare-and-swap), reduce the need for locks and minimize the risk of deadlocks.

2. Race Conditions

A race condition occurs when two or more threads access shared data simultaneously, and at least one of the threads modifies the data. If the threads' operations are not properly synchronized, this can lead to unpredictable or incorrect behavior.

Example of a Race Condition

Consider a counter variable accessed by multiple threads:

- Thread A reads the value of the counter (e.g., 5).
- Before Thread A updates the counter, Thread B also reads the counter value (still 5).
- Both threads increment the counter and write the value back (6), instead of incrementing it twice (to 7).

In this scenario, the final value of the counter is incorrect because the two threads interfered with each other's operations.

Avoiding Race Conditions

- **Synchronization Mechanisms**:
- Use synchronization primitives like mutexes, locks, or synchronized blocks (in Java/Kotlin) to ensure that only one thread accesses critical sections of code at a time. This prevents multiple threads from modifying shared data simultaneously.
- **Atomic Operations**:
- Atomic operations are indivisible actions that guarantee the operation is completed fully before another thread can intervene. Programming languages often provide atomic classes (e.g., AtomicInteger in Java) to handle simple operations without needing full synchronization.

- **Immutable Objects**:
- Immutable objects cannot be modified after creation. By using immutable objects, developers eliminate the risk of race conditions, as multiple threads can safely read the object without conflicts.
- **Thread-Safe Data Structures**:
- Many programming languages offer thread-safe data structures (e.g., ConcurrentHashMap in Java) that manage synchronization internally, allowing multiple threads to access and modify data safely.

Concurrency in Mobile Platforms

Concurrency in iOS (GCD and Operation Queues)

I n iOS, concurrency is managed primarily through **Grand Central Dispatch (GCD)** and **Operation Queues**, both of which provide powerful and flexible ways to perform tasks asynchronously, keeping the main thread free to handle user interactions and update the user interface. Understanding how these tools work is crucial for building responsive and efficient iOS applications.

Grand Central Dispatch (GCD)

GCD is a low-level API provided by Apple that allows developers to execute code concurrently by dispatching tasks to queues managed by the system. It abstracts away the complexity of creating and managing threads directly, making it simpler to perform operations in the background while maintaining app responsiveness.

Key Concepts of GCD

1. **Queues**:

- GCD uses *dispatch queues* to manage tasks. Queues are responsible for executing blocks of code (tasks) either serially (one after another) or concurrently (multiple tasks at the same time).
- **Types of Queues:**

- **Main Queue**: A serial queue that runs on the main thread. This queue is used for UI updates and must never be blocked.
- **Global Queues**: Concurrent queues provided by the system that run tasks in parallel. They come with different Quality of Service (QoS) levels such as userInteractive, userInitiated, utility, and background to prioritize tasks based on their importance and resource requirements.
- **Custom Queues**: Developers can create their own serial or concurrent queues to manage tasks according to the specific needs of the app.

1. **Dispatching Tasks**:

- GCD allows developers to dispatch tasks synchronously (sync) or asynchronously (async):
- **Synchronous Dispatch (sync)**: The task runs on the current thread and blocks it until the task completes. It's generally used when you need to ensure that a task finishes before moving on to the next operation.
- **Asynchronous Dispatch (async)**: The task is dispatched to a queue and runs independently of the current thread, allowing the app to remain responsive. This is the most common method for performing background tasks.

Example of Using GCD in iOS (Swift)

```swift
Copy code
// Dispatching a background task to fetch data asynchronously
DispatchQueue.global(qos: .userInitiated).async {
    // Perform network request or intensive computation
    let data = fetchDataFromServer()

    // Update the UI on the main thread after fetching data
    DispatchQueue.main.async {
        updateUI(with: data)
    }
}
```

```
}
```

- In this example, a task is dispatched to a global queue with a userInitiated QoS, which prioritizes the task because it is important for user interaction. The network request runs asynchronously, and once it completes, the UI is updated on the main queue.

Quality of Service (QoS) Levels
GCD provides QoS levels to prioritize tasks:

- **User Interactive**: For tasks that directly affect user interactions and should run immediately (e.g., animations).
- **User Initiated**: For tasks initiated by the user that are not immediately needed but should complete quickly (e.g., loading data).
- **Utility**: For tasks that involve longer processing times, such as downloading files or syncing.
- **Background**: For tasks that don't require immediate attention, like prefetching data or maintenance tasks.

Operation Queues
Operation Queues provide a higher-level abstraction over GCD, offering more control and flexibility when managing concurrent tasks. They are built on top of GCD but provide additional features such as task dependencies, cancellation, and prioritization.
Key Concepts of Operation Queues

1. **Operations**:

- Operations are encapsulated units of work that can be executed concurrently or serially. iOS provides the Operation class and its subclass BlockOperation, which allows developers to create and manage operations easily.

- Operations are more versatile than GCD blocks, as they can be paused, resumed, canceled, or set with dependencies.

1. **Operation Queues**:

- An OperationQueue manages the execution of multiple operations. Developers can set the queue as serial (only one operation at a time) or concurrent (multiple operations simultaneously).
- Operations added to a queue can have dependencies, meaning one operation will not start until another completes. This is particularly useful for tasks that need to occur in a specific order.

Example of Using Operation Queues in iOS (Swift)

```swift
Copy code
let queue = OperationQueue()

let operation1 = BlockOperation {
    // Perform the first task
    print("Task 1 running")
}

let operation2 = BlockOperation {
    // Perform the second task
    print("Task 2 running")
}

// Setting a dependency: operation2 will not start until
operation1 finishes
operation2.addDependency(operation1)

queue.addOperations([operation1, operation2], waitUntilFinished:
false)
```

- In this example, operation2 is set to depend on operation1, ensuring that operation1 completes before operation2 begins.

When to Use Operation Queues vs. GCD

- **GCD** is ideal for lightweight, straightforward tasks where you do not need much control beyond dispatching work asynchronously.
- **Operation Queues** are more suitable when you need to manage complex task relationships, such as dependencies, cancellation, and prioritization.

Concurrency in Android (Threads, AsyncTask, Executors)

In Android, concurrency is managed using various tools and frameworks such as **Threads**, **AsyncTask** (now deprecated), and **Executors**. Each provides different levels of abstraction and flexibility for handling background tasks efficiently.

Threads in Android

Threads are the most basic unit of concurrency in Android. They allow developers to execute code asynchronously, ensuring that the main thread remains responsive. However, directly managing threads requires careful handling to avoid issues like thread leaks or synchronization problems.

Using Threads in Android (Kotlin)

```kotlin
Copy code
Thread {
    // Perform a background task
    val data = fetchDataFromServer()

    // Update the UI on the main thread
    runOnUiThread {
        updateUI(data)
    }
}.start()
```

- In this example, a new thread is created to perform a network request, and runOnUiThread is used to update the UI, ensuring that all UI modifications happen on the main thread.

Challenges of Using Threads Directly

- **Complexity**: Managing multiple threads manually can be error-prone, especially when ensuring threads terminate correctly or when accessing shared resources.
- **No Built-in Lifecycle Management**: Threads do not automatically manage themselves based on the activity lifecycle, which can lead to memory leaks if they are not properly handled.

AsyncTask (Deprecated)

AsyncTask was a common tool for handling background operations like network requests or database access. However, it has been deprecated due to its limitations and challenges, such as lifecycle management issues and poor scalability.

Basic Structure of AsyncTask

```java
Copy code
private class MyAsyncTask extends AsyncTask<Void, Void, String> {

    @Override
    protected String doInBackground(Void... params) {
        // Perform background computation
        return fetchDataFromServer();
    }

    @Override
    protected void onPostExecute(String result) {
        // Update UI with the result
        updateUI(result);
    }
```

```
}
```

- The doInBackground method runs asynchronously, and onPostExecute updates the UI on the main thread after the background task completes.

Limitations of AsyncTask

- **Lifecycle Issues**: AsyncTask instances are not automatically tied to the lifecycle of the activity or fragment, leading to potential memory leaks if the task outlives the activity.
- **Limited Flexibility**: AsyncTask is designed for short, simple tasks and may not handle complex use cases or large numbers of tasks efficiently.

Executors in Android

The **Executor** framework is a more modern and flexible approach to managing threads and tasks. It abstracts away much of the complexity of manually handling threads and offers a pool of threads for executing tasks concurrently.

Types of Executors

1. **SingleThreadExecutor**:

- Executes tasks sequentially in a single background thread, useful when tasks need to run one after another.

1. **FixedThreadPool**:

- Manages a fixed number of threads that execute tasks concurrently. It's ideal for handling multiple tasks in parallel while keeping the number of threads limited.

1. **CachedThreadPool**:

- Dynamically creates new threads as needed but reuses previously created threads when they are available. This is useful for handling tasks that vary in frequency and length.

Example: Using an ExecutorService in Android (Kotlin)

```kotlin
Copy code
val executor = Executors.newSingleThreadExecutor()

executor.execute {
    // Perform a background task
    val data = fetchDataFromServer()

    // Update the UI on the main thread
    runOnUiThread {
        updateUI(data)
    }
}
```

- In this example, an ExecutorService is created with a single thread, and a background task is executed. The runOnUiThread method ensures that UI updates occur on the main thread.

Advantages of Executors

- **Lifecycle Awareness**: Executors offer better management of resources compared to direct thread usage. They can be integrated with Android's lifecycle components for more efficient task management.
- **Thread Pool Management**: Executors handle thread creation and reuse automatically, reducing overhead and improving performance.

Kotlin Coroutines: The Modern Approach

Kotlin Coroutines provide a more intuitive and powerful way to manage concurrency in Android. Coroutines allow developers to write asynchronous code in a sequential style, making it easier to read and manage.

Example of a Kotlin Coroutine

```kotlin
Copy code
GlobalScope.launch {
    val result = fetchDataFromApi() // Runs on a background thread
    withContext(Dispatchers.Main) {
        updateUI(result) // Runs on the main thread
    }
}
```

- **launch**: Starts a new coroutine that runs asynchronously.
- **withContext(Dispatchers.Main)**: Switches the coroutine's context to the main thread for UI updates.
- Coroutines handle lifecycle management more gracefully when used with Android's ViewModel and LifecycleScope, ensuring that background tasks do not leak resources when activities or fragments are destroyed

Understanding Framework-Specific Concurrency APIs (Kotlin Coroutines, Swift Async/Await)

Modern mobile development frameworks like Kotlin for Android and Swift for iOS have introduced powerful concurrency APIs that simplify writing and managing asynchronous code. These APIs, such as Kotlin Coroutines and Swift's async/await, allow developers to write code in a sequential style while still taking advantage of the benefits of concurrency. This approach significantly improves code readability and maintainability.

Kotlin Coroutines

Kotlin Coroutines are a powerful concurrency framework introduced in Kotlin for managing asynchronous programming in Android. They provide a structured, lightweight way to handle tasks like network requests, file operations, and background processing without blocking the main thread.

Key Concepts of Kotlin Coroutines

1. **Coroutine**:

- A coroutine is a lightweight thread that can be suspended and resumed later. Unlike traditional threads, coroutines are managed by the Kotlin runtime, making them more efficient and less resource-intensive.

1. **Coroutine Builders**:

- Coroutines are started using coroutine builders, such as:
- **launch**: Starts a coroutine that does not return a value. It is typically used when the result of the operation is not needed.
- **async**: Starts a coroutine that returns a Deferred object, which represents a future result. The result can be awaited using the await() function.

1. **Dispatchers**:

- Coroutines run on dispatchers, which determine the thread or pool of threads used:
- **Dispatchers.Main**: Runs tasks on the main thread, suitable for UI updates.
- **Dispatchers.IO**: Optimized for I/O operations such as database access or network calls.
- **Dispatchers.Default**: Used for CPU-intensive tasks like sorting large lists or performing complex calculations.
- **Dispatchers.Unconfined**: Starts tasks in the caller's context but can be useful for certain use cases where flexibility is needed.

1. **Suspending Functions**:

- A suspending function is a function that can be paused and resumed later, allowing coroutines to manage asynchronous tasks without blocking threads. These functions are marked with the suspend keyword and can be called only from other suspending functions or within coroutines.

Example of Kotlin Coroutines in Android

```kotlin
Copy code
fun fetchData() {
    GlobalScope.launch(Dispatchers.IO) {
        val result = fetchDataFromApi() // Suspended until the
        network call completes
        withContext(Dispatchers.Main) {
            updateUI(result) // Switches to the main thread for UI
            updates
        }
    }
}
```

- **Explanation**:
- GlobalScope.launch: Launches a coroutine in the global scope on an I/O-optimized dispatcher.
- fetchDataFromApi(): A suspending function that performs a network call.
- withContext(Dispatchers.Main): Switches the coroutine's context to the main thread for updating the UI.

Benefits of Kotlin Coroutines

- **Sequential Style**: Coroutines allow developers to write asynchronous code in a sequential style, improving readability and maintainability.

- **Structured Concurrency**: Coroutines provide structured concurrency, meaning that they are tied to a lifecycle (e.g., a ViewModel or activity), reducing the risk of memory leaks.
- **Lightweight**: Unlike traditional threads, coroutines are lightweight, allowing thousands of them to run concurrently without significant overhead.

Advanced Features

- **Coroutine Scopes**: Scopes control the lifecycle of coroutines, ensuring they are canceled when the associated lifecycle component (e.g., activity or fragment) is destroyed. Scopes like viewModelScope and lifecycleScope help integrate coroutines with Android architecture components.
- **Flows**: Flows represent a stream of asynchronous data and are used for reactive programming, allowing developers to handle data streams such as live data updates from databases or APIs.

Swift Async/Await

Introduced in Swift 5.5, async/await brings a modern and efficient way to handle concurrency in iOS development. This API simplifies writing asynchronous code by enabling developers to write code in a synchronous style while still managing tasks asynchronously.

Key Concepts of Swift Async/Await

1. **async Function**:

- An async function is a function that can suspend execution to await the completion of another task. These functions must be called from within other async functions or coroutines.

1. **await Keyword**:

- The await keyword is used within an async function to pause its execution

69

until another asynchronous task completes. The function resumes once the awaited task finishes.

1. **Task**:

- A Task represents a unit of asynchronous work. Developers can create tasks using the Task initializer to run concurrent operations.
- **Task Groups**: Allow for managing multiple tasks concurrently and collecting their results.

Example of Swift Async/Await in iOS

```swift
Copy code
func fetchData() async {
    do {
        let result = try await fetchDataFromServer() //
        Asynchronous network call
        await updateUI(with: result) // Ensures UI update happens
        on the main thread
    } catch {
        print("Error fetching data: \(error)")
    }
}
```

- **Explanation**:
- The fetchData function is marked as async, indicating it can be paused to wait for other asynchronous operations.
- await fetchDataFromServer(): Calls an asynchronous function that fetches data from a server.
- await updateUI(with: result): Updates the UI asynchronously, ensuring that it runs on the main thread.

Benefits of Swift Async/Await

- **Simplified Asynchronous Code**: async/await makes asynchronous code easier to read and write, resembling synchronous code structure.
- **Error Handling**: Integrates seamlessly with Swift's error-handling system, making it easier to manage errors in asynchronous code.
- **Performance**: The new concurrency model in Swift is optimized for performance, leveraging lightweight, managed tasks that are more efficient than traditional threads.

Advanced Features

- **Actors**: Swift's concurrency model introduces actors, which provide data isolation and synchronization, ensuring that mutable state is safely accessed across concurrent tasks.
- **Structured Concurrency**: Tasks in Swift are structured, meaning that parent tasks manage the lifecycle of their child tasks, reducing the risk of memory leaks and ensuring proper cancellation.

Cross-Platform Concurrency Considerations (Flutter, React Native)

Cross-platform frameworks like Flutter and React Native provide tools and libraries that abstract platform-specific concurrency details, allowing developers to implement asynchronous code that works across both iOS and Android. These frameworks offer flexibility but come with their own set of challenges and considerations.

Concurrency in Flutter

Flutter, developed by Google, uses the Dart programming language, which offers its own concurrency model based on **async/await** and **Isolates**.

Key Concurrency Concepts in Flutter

1. **Dart's async/await**:

- Dart supports async/await, similar to Swift and Kotlin, for managing asynchronous code. This syntax allows developers to write code that waits for operations like network requests or file I/O without blocking the main thread.

1. **Isolates**:

- Isolates are Dart's way of handling concurrency. They are independent memory spaces and threads, enabling true parallelism. Unlike traditional threads, Isolates do not share memory, so data must be transferred between them using message passing.
- **Use Case**: Isolates are used for CPU-intensive tasks like image processing or complex computations that need to run in parallel without affecting the UI.

Example of Using async/await in Flutter

```dart
Copy code
Future<void> fetchData() async {
  try {
    final result = await fetchDataFromApi(); // Asynchronous API
    call
    setState(() {
      _data = result; // Update the UI
    });
  } catch (error) {
    print('Error fetching data: $error');
  }
}
```

- **Explanation**: The function fetchData is asynchronous, and it fetches data from an API. The await keyword pauses execution until the API call completes, and then the UI is updated with setState.

Example of Using Isolates in Flutter

```dart
Copy code
import 'dart:isolate';

void longRunningTask(SendPort sendPort) {
  // Perform intensive computation
  int result = computeIntensiveTask();
  sendPort.send(result);
}

void runTask() async {
  final receivePort = ReceivePort();
  await Isolate.spawn(longRunningTask, receivePort.sendPort);

  receivePort.listen((message) {
    // Process the result from the isolate
    print('Result from isolate: $message');
  });
}
```

- **Explanation**: In this example, an Isolate is used to run a CPU-intensive task independently of the main thread. The SendPort and ReceivePort are used for communication between the main thread and the Isolate.

Concurrency in React Native

React Native uses JavaScript's asynchronous model, relying heavily on **Promises, async/await**, and **native modules** for concurrency.

Key Concurrency Concepts in React Native

1. **Promises**:

- JavaScript's Promise API allows developers to handle asynchronous operations such as API calls, file access, or database queries. Promises can be chained to handle sequences of asynchronous events, making it easier to manage complex tasks.

1. **async/await**:

- async/await is a modern JavaScript syntax for handling asynchronous code. It simplifies the use of Promises by allowing asynchronous code to be written in a more readable and synchronous-like manner.

1. **Native Modules**:

- For CPU-intensive operations or tasks that require true parallelism, React Native allows developers to write native code in Java (for Android) or Objective-C/Swift (for iOS). These native modules can then be called from JavaScript, enabling developers to take advantage of platform-specific concurrency features.

Example of Using async/await in React Native

```javascript
Copy code
async function fetchData() {
    try {
        const response = await
        fetch('https://api.example.com/data');
        const result = await response.json();
        setData(result);
    } catch (error) {
        console.error('Error fetching data:', error);
    }
}
```

- **Explanation**: The fetchData function uses async/await to make an API call asynchronously. It waits for the API response and parses the data without blocking the UI.

Example of Using a Native Module for Concurrency

```javascript
Copy code
import { NativeModules } from 'react-native';
const { MyNativeModule } = NativeModules;

MyNativeModule.performLongRunningTask((result) => {
    console.log('Result from native module:', result);
});
```

- **Explanation**: This example shows how a React Native app can offload intensive tasks to native code. The JavaScript code calls a native module, which performs the operation in parallel using the platform's concurrency capabilities.

Cross-Platform Considerations

1. **Performance Overhead**:

- Cross-platform frameworks abstract platform-specific concurrency details, which can introduce a slight overhead compared to native implementations. Developers should be aware of this when dealing with resource-intensive tasks and consider using native modules for optimized performance.

1. **Consistency Across Platforms**:

- Ensuring that asynchronous code behaves consistently on both iOS and Android can be challenging. Testing across multiple devices and platforms is crucial to verify that concurrency implementations perform reliably.

1. **Integration with Platform-Specific APIs**:

- While Flutter and React Native offer their own concurrency models, there are cases where developers need to tap into platform-specific APIs for advanced functionality. Understanding how to integrate these APIs while maintaining cross-platform compatibility is essential for building robust applications.

Implementing Multithreading in Mobile Apps

Creating and Managing Threads in iOS

I n iOS, while higher-level concurrency abstractions like **Grand Central Dispatch (GCD)** and **Operation Queues** are commonly used, there are scenarios where developers may need to create and manage threads directly. This approach provides more control over how tasks are executed and is useful for understanding the fundamental mechanics of concurrency in iOS.

1. Understanding Threads in iOS

A **thread** is a basic unit of execution within a process. In iOS, when an app is launched, a main thread is created to handle the app's user interface (UI) and user interactions. Additional threads can be created for performing tasks concurrently, such as network operations, file handling, or other background processing, without blocking the main thread.

The iOS operating system uses **POSIX threads (pthreads)** at a low level, but working with them directly is uncommon due to their complexity. Instead, iOS developers typically use NSThread, which provides a simpler interface for creating and managing threads.

2. Using NSThread

NSThread is a class in iOS that allows developers to create and manage threads more easily than dealing with raw pthreads. While it's not as high-level as GCD or Operation Queues, it gives more control over thread behavior and lifecycle.

Creating and Starting a Thread with NSThread

To create a new thread, you instantiate an NSThread object and specify the target method and the object that will execute on that thread. Here's a simple example:

```swift
Copy code
let newThread = Thread {
    // The code to run on the new thread
    print("This is running on a background thread.")
    performHeavyCalculation()
}

// Start the thread
newThread.start()
```

- **Explanation**:
- An instance of Thread is created with a closure (block) that contains the code to execute.
- The start() method launches the thread, and the code within the closure runs on that new thread.

Creating a Thread with a Selector

Another way to create a thread is by using a selector method:

```swift
Copy code
let newThread = Thread(target: self, selector:
#selector(doBackgroundWork), object: nil)
newThread.start()

@objc func doBackgroundWork() {
```

```
    print("Doing work on a background thread.")
    // Perform your background task here
}
```

- **Explanation**:
- The Thread instance is initialized with a target object (self), a selector (#selector(doBackgroundWork)), and an optional object parameter (nil in this case).
- The method doBackgroundWork is marked with @objc because it is used as a selector.

3. **Controlling Thread Behavior**

NSThread offers several methods for controlling thread behavior:

- **Pausing a Thread**:
- You can pause a thread using Thread.sleep(forTimeInterval:) or Thread.sleep(until:) to temporarily halt its execution. This is useful when you need to delay certain actions within the thread.

```
swift
Copy code
Thread.sleep(forTimeInterval: 2.0) // Pauses the thread for 2
seconds
```

- **Exiting a Thread**:
- A thread can be stopped using exit(). However, this should be done carefully to avoid leaving resources in an inconsistent state.

```swift
Copy code
if Thread.current.isCancelled {
    Thread.exit()
}
```

- **Priority Management**:
- NSThread allows setting the priority of threads using the threadPriority property, with values ranging from 0.0 (lowest priority) to 1.0 (highest priority).

```swift
Copy code
newThread.threadPriority = 0.5 // Set the thread priority to medium
```

4. Synchronization with Locks

When multiple threads access shared resources, synchronization is necessary to prevent race conditions. NSThread provides locks (NSLock) to manage access to shared resources:

```swift
Copy code
let lock = NSLock()

func safeMethod() {
    lock.lock()
    // Critical section: modify shared resource
    print("This code is thread-safe.")
    lock.unlock()
}
```

- **Explanation**:

- NSLock ensures that only one thread at a time can access the critical section, preventing concurrent access and ensuring thread safety.

5. **When to Use NSThread**

While NSThread offers control over thread creation and behavior, it's not often the preferred choice in modern iOS development due to the complexity of managing threads manually. Higher-level abstractions like GCD and Operation Queues provide more efficient and safer ways to manage concurrency. However, understanding NSThread is valuable for scenarios where direct control over threads is necessary, such as when building low-level libraries or optimizing specific performance-critical tasks.

Thread Pools and Executors in Android

In Android, managing threads directly can be complex, so the platform provides higher-level abstractions like **Executors** and **Thread Pools** to simplify concurrency management. These abstractions allow developers to handle multiple tasks efficiently by managing a pool of reusable threads.

1. **Understanding Thread Pools**

A **thread pool** is a collection of pre-created threads that can be reused for executing tasks. Instead of creating a new thread for every task (which can be expensive and inefficient), a thread pool reuses available threads, reducing overhead and improving performance.

- **Benefits of Using Thread Pools**:
- **Efficiency**: Reusing threads minimizes the cost of thread creation and destruction.
- **Resource Management**: Limits the number of concurrent threads, preventing system overload.
- **Task Queuing**: Tasks are queued and executed as threads become available, ensuring that no task is missed.

2. **Executors Framework**

81

The **Executors** framework in Android provides a simple and efficient way to manage thread pools. It abstracts the creation and management of threads, allowing developers to focus on task execution rather than thread lifecycle management.

Types of Executors

The Executors framework provides several implementations based on the use case:

1. **SingleThreadExecutor**:

- This executor maintains a single background thread for executing tasks sequentially.
- **Use Case**: Suitable for tasks that need to run one after another, such as logging events or maintaining a sequence of network requests.

```kotlin
Copy code
val executor = Executors.newSingleThreadExecutor()

executor.execute {
    // Task to be executed in the background
    performTask()
}
```

1. **FixedThreadPool**:

- Manages a fixed number of threads in the pool. If all threads are busy, new tasks are queued until a thread becomes available.
- **Use Case**: Suitable for applications with a predictable number of tasks that can be executed in parallel.

```kotlin
Copy code
val executor = Executors.newFixedThreadPool(3) // Pool with 3
threads

executor.execute {
    // Task to be executed in the background
    performTask()
}
```

1. CachedThreadPool:

- Creates new threads as needed and reuses existing ones when available. It has no fixed size, so it grows and shrinks based on the number of tasks.
- **Use Case**: Ideal for short-lived tasks that vary in frequency and duration. It's efficient for handling bursts of requests but can be resource-intensive if not managed properly.

```kotlin
Copy code
val executor = Executors.newCachedThreadPool()

executor.execute {
    // Task to be executed in the background
    performTask()
}
```

1. ScheduledThreadPool:

- Supports executing tasks after a delay or at fixed intervals. It is useful for scheduling periodic tasks like data syncing or performing maintenance operations.

- **Use Case**: Suitable for tasks that need to be executed periodically or after a certain delay.

```kotlin
Copy code
val scheduledExecutor = Executors.newScheduledThreadPool(2)

scheduledExecutor.scheduleAtFixedRate({
    // Task to be executed periodically
    performScheduledTask()
}, 0, 1, TimeUnit.SECONDS)
```

- **Explanation**: The above code schedules a task to run every second, with no initial delay.

3. Managing Task Execution with ExecutorService

The ExecutorService interface extends the basic Executor framework, providing methods for managing the lifecycle of threads and tasks:

1. Shutting Down Executors:

- Executors can be shut down using shutdown() or shutdownNow().
- shutdown(): Stops accepting new tasks but allows previously submitted tasks to complete.
- shutdownNow(): Attempts to stop all actively executing tasks and cancels pending tasks.

```kotlin
Copy code
executor.shutdown() // Graceful shutdown
```

1. Handling Callable Tasks:

- Unlike Runnable, which does not return a result, Callable tasks return a result or throw an exception. The result can be retrieved using the Future object.

```kotlin
Copy code
val executor = Executors.newFixedThreadPool(2)

val future: Future<Int> = executor.submit(Callable {
    // Perform computation and return result
    return@Callable performComputation()
})

try {
    val result = future.get() // Blocks until the result is
    available
    println("Computation result: $result")
} catch (e: InterruptedException) {
    e.printStackTrace()
} catch (e: ExecutionException) {
    e.printStackTrace()
}
```

- **Explanation**: In this example, a Callable task is submitted to the executor, and its result is obtained using Future.get(). This approach is useful when you need to execute tasks that produce results.

4. Handling Thread Pools with Kotlin Coroutines

In modern Android development, Kotlin Coroutines provide an alternative to traditional executors and thread pools. Coroutines offer a structured and lightweight approach to concurrency, allowing developers to manage tasks without the need for explicitly managing thread pools.

Example of Using Coroutines as an Alternative to Executors

```kotlin
kotlin
Copy code
import kotlinx.coroutines.*

fun performCoroutineTask() {
    GlobalScope.launch(Dispatchers.IO) {
        val result = performNetworkRequest()
        withContext(Dispatchers.Main) {
            updateUI(result)
        }
    }
}
```

- **Explanation**:
- The coroutine runs in the IO dispatcher, optimized for I/O operations.
- The result is processed on the main thread using withContext(Dispatchers.Main).

5. When to Use Executors vs. Coroutines

- **Executors**:
- Suitable for scenarios where you need a traditional thread pool model, such as handling multiple, simple tasks concurrently.
- Useful when you need fine-grained control over task scheduling, prioritization, and thread management.
- **Kotlin Coroutines**:
- A modern and preferred approach in Android development for handling concurrency. Coroutines offer lifecycle-aware features, which integrate well with Android architecture components, reducing memory leaks and providing a more seamless development experience.

Effective thread management is essential for building responsive and efficient mobile applications. Whether developing for iOS or Android, adhering to best practices helps avoid common concurrency issues such as deadlocks, race conditions, and memory leaks. Here are some best practices for managing threads effectively:

1. **Avoid Blocking the Main Thread**
   - The main thread is responsible for user interface (UI) updates and handling user interactions. Blocking it with long-running tasks (e.g., network requests, file operations, or intensive calculations) can cause the application to become unresponsive and lead to a poor user experience.
   - **Solution**: Offload any long-running or resource-intensive tasks to background threads using frameworks like **Grand Central Dispatch (GCD)** in iOS or **Executors/Coroutines** in Android.

2. **Use High-Level Abstractions (GCD, Operation Queues, Coroutines)**

   - Instead of managing threads manually, use high-level abstractions like **GCD** and **Operation Queues** in iOS or **Executors** and **Kotlin Coroutines** in Android. These tools handle thread creation, scheduling, and execution efficiently, reducing the complexity and potential errors associated with manual thread management.
   - These abstractions also provide built-in features for error handling, task cancellation, and lifecycle management, ensuring that background tasks are executed safely.

3. **Keep Background Tasks Lightweight**

   - Background tasks should be as lightweight as possible to avoid exhausting system resources. Heavy tasks that take a long time should be broken down into smaller units or handled incrementally to avoid blocking background threads for extended periods.

- Use techniques like **batch processing** for tasks such as syncing data or reading files incrementally, ensuring other tasks in the queue can continue executing without waiting too long.

4. Implement Task Cancellation and Timeouts

- Tasks running on background threads should support cancellation and timeouts, particularly for network operations and other potentially long-running processes. This is important for maintaining app performance and preventing unnecessary resource usage.
- In iOS, tasks dispatched with GCD can be canceled using **Operation Queues** with dependencies and cancellation flags. In Android, **Kotlin Coroutines** provide the cancel() method, and ExecutorService tasks can be canceled using the Future.cancel() method.

5. Use Thread-Safe Data Structures

- Accessing shared resources from multiple threads without proper synchronization can lead to race conditions and data corruption. Use thread-safe data structures (e.g., ConcurrentHashMap in Java) or synchronization primitives (e.g., NSLock in iOS) to manage shared resources safely.
- Another approach is to use **immutable objects**, which prevent data modification once created, making them inherently thread-safe.

6. Use Lifecycles and Scopes for Thread Management

- In Android, using lifecycle-aware components like ViewModel with viewModelScope or lifecycleScope helps manage coroutines and threads based on the lifecycle of activities and fragments. This reduces memory leaks and ensures that background tasks are automatically canceled when the associated component is destroyed.
- In iOS, tie tasks to specific lifecycle events (e.g., viewDidAppear or viewWillDisappear) and make use of Operation objects that can be easily

canceled when the view controller is no longer active.

7. Test for Thread Safety

- Test the application thoroughly for thread safety, particularly when accessing shared resources. Use tools like **Instruments** in iOS or **Android Profiler** to analyze thread behavior, detect potential deadlocks, and optimize performance.
- Simulate various conditions, such as low memory, high CPU usage, and network delays, to identify and resolve concurrency issues that may not be apparent under normal conditions.

8. Use Background Task APIs for Long-Running Operations

- For tasks that need to continue running even when the app is in the background (e.g., uploading files or fetching data), use background task APIs provided by the platforms. In iOS, **URLSession** with background configuration can be used for long-running network tasks, while Android provides **WorkManager** for managing deferrable background work.

Examples: Running Network Operations and File Operations on Background Threads

Properly managing background tasks for network and file operations ensures the application remains responsive and performant. Here are examples of how to perform these operations on background threads in iOS and Android:

1. Running Network Operations on Background Threads

Network operations, such as API calls or downloading files, should always run on background threads to prevent blocking the UI.

iOS Example: Using GCD for Network Operations

```swift
swift
Copy code
func fetchDataFromServer() {
    DispatchQueue.global(qos: .background).async {
        guard let url = URL(string:
        "https://api.example.com/data") else { return }
        do {
            let data = try Data(contentsOf: url)
            DispatchQueue.main.async {
                // Update the UI with the fetched data
                self.updateUI(with: data)
            }
        } catch {
            print("Error fetching data: \(error)")
        }
    }
}

func updateUI(with data: Data) {
    // Parse and update the UI based on the fetched data
}
```

- **Explanation**:
- The network request runs asynchronously on a global background queue (DispatchQueue.global).
- Once the data is fetched, it switches back to the main queue (DispatchQueue.main) to update the UI, ensuring all UI changes occur on the main thread.

Android Example: Using Kotlin Coroutines for Network Operations

```kotlin
kotlin
Copy code
import kotlinx.coroutines.*

fun fetchDataFromServer() {
```

```
    GlobalScope.launch(Dispatchers.IO) {
        try {
            val result = fetchDataFromApi() // Network call
            withContext(Dispatchers.Main) {
                updateUI(result) // Update UI on main thread
            }
        } catch (e: Exception) {
            e.printStackTrace()
        }
    }
}

suspend fun fetchDataFromApi(): String {
    // Simulate network request and return result
    delay(1000) // Simulating network delay
    return "Data from server"
}

fun updateUI(data: String) {
    // Update UI with the data received from the network
}
```

- **Explanation**:
- The coroutine runs on the IO dispatcher, optimized for network and I/O operations.
- withContext(Dispatchers.Main) switches the execution to the main thread for UI updates.
- This approach ensures that the network call does not block the main thread and keeps the UI responsive.

2. Running File Operations on Background Threads

File operations, such as reading and writing large files, should also be performed on background threads to avoid slowing down the UI.

iOS Example: Using GCD for File Operations

```swift
swift
Copy code
func readFile() {
    DispatchQueue.global(qos: .utility).async {
        let filePath = "/path/to/your/file.txt"
        do {
            let fileContents = try String(contentsOfFile:
            filePath, encoding: .utf8)
            DispatchQueue.main.async {
                // Update UI with the file contents
                self.displayFileContents(fileContents)
            }
        } catch {
            print("Error reading file: \(error)")
        }
    }
}

func displayFileContents(_ contents: String) {
    // Display file contents on the UI
}
```

- **Explanation**:
- The file read operation is dispatched to a global background queue (DispatchQueue.global with .utility QoS) to perform file reading asynchronously.
- After reading the file, the main queue is used to update the UI, ensuring all changes are made on the main thread.

Android Example: Using Executors for File Operations

```kotlin
kotlin
Copy code
import java.util.concurrent.Executors

val executor = Executors.newSingleThreadExecutor()
```

```kotlin
fun readFile() {
    executor.execute {
        try {
            val fileContents = readFromFile("path/to/file.txt")
            runOnUiThread {
                displayFileContents(fileContents)
            }
        } catch (e: Exception) {
            e.printStackTrace()
        }
    }
}

fun readFromFile(filePath: String): String {
    // Simulate reading from a file
    return "File contents"
}

fun displayFileContents(contents: String) {
    // Update the UI with the file contents
}
```

- **Explanation**:
- A single-thread executor is used to run the file read operation in the background.
- runOnUiThread is used to ensure the UI is updated on the main thread, maintaining thread safety.

Alternative in Android: Using Kotlin Coroutines for File Operations

```kotlin
kotlin
Copy code
fun readFile() {
    GlobalScope.launch(Dispatchers.IO) {
        try {
```

```
            val fileContents = readFromFile("path/to/file.txt")
            withContext(Dispatchers.Main) {
                displayFileContents(fileContents)
            }
        } catch (e: Exception) {
            e.printStackTrace()
        }
    }
}

suspend fun readFromFile(filePath: String): String {
    // Simulate file read delay
    delay(500)
    return "File contents"
}
```

- **Explanation**:
- The coroutine runs on the IO dispatcher for the file operation, ensuring that the main thread remains free for UI updates.
- Switching to Dispatchers.Main using withContext ensures the UI update happens safely on the main thread.

Using Queues and Executors for Task Management

Working with Queues in iOS (Main Queue, Global Queues, Custom Queues)

I n iOS, **Grand Central Dispatch (GCD)** provides a powerful and efficient mechanism for managing concurrency using queues. Queues are responsible for organizing tasks and executing them either serially (one after another) or concurrently (multiple tasks at the same time). GCD abstracts the complexity of thread management, making it easier to run tasks asynchronously and keep the main thread responsive. Understanding how to use different types of queues—**Main Queue, Global Queues**, and **Custom Queues**—is essential for building responsive and performant iOS applications.

1. **Main Queue**

The **Main Queue** is a special serial queue that runs on the main thread. It is used for executing tasks that update the user interface (UI) and handle user interactions. Since all UI-related tasks must be performed on the main thread to avoid conflicts and crashes, developers frequently use the main queue for such operations.

Characteristics of the Main Queue:

• **Serial Execution**: The main queue executes tasks one at a time, ensuring that only one UI operation occurs at any given moment.

- **Main Thread**: The main queue is tied to the main thread of the application, which is responsible for rendering the UI and processing user events.

Example: Using the Main Queue in iOS

```swift
Copy code
func updateUI() {
    DispatchQueue.main.async {
        // Update UI elements
        self.label.text = "Data Loaded"
        self.activityIndicator.stopAnimating()
    }
}
```

- **Explanation**: The DispatchQueue.main.async method schedules the task asynchronously on the main queue. This ensures that the UI update (e.g., changing the label's text or stopping an activity indicator) occurs on the main thread, preventing potential crashes.

2. Global Queues

Global Queues are concurrent queues provided by the system for executing tasks in the background. These queues are shared across the application and come with different **Quality of Service (QoS)** levels that prioritize tasks based on their importance and resource needs.

Characteristics of Global Queues:

- **Concurrent Execution**: Global queues run tasks concurrently, allowing multiple tasks to execute simultaneously.
- **System-Managed**: These queues are managed by the system, and tasks are scheduled based on available resources and priorities.
- **QoS Levels**: GCD provides several QoS levels for global queues:

- **userInteractive**: For tasks that directly affect user interactions and should complete immediately (e.g., animations).
- **userInitiated**: For tasks initiated by the user that need to complete quickly but do not immediately affect the UI (e.g., loading data after a button click).
- **utility**: For long-running tasks that do not require immediate results, such as downloading files or processing large amounts of data.
- **background**: For tasks that run in the background without user interaction, such as pre-fetching data or syncing files.

Example: Using a Global Queue in iOS

```swift
Copy code
func fetchData() {
    DispatchQueue.global(qos: .userInitiated).async {
        // Perform a network request or heavy computation
        let data = fetchDataFromServer()

        DispatchQueue.main.async {
            // Update UI with fetched data
            self.updateUI(with: data)
        }
    }
}
```

- **Explanation**: The task is dispatched to a global queue with a userInitiated QoS, indicating that the task is important but not critical for immediate user interaction. The network request runs asynchronously, and once the data is fetched, the DispatchQueue.main.async method is used to update the UI on the main thread.

3. Custom Queues

Custom queues allow developers to create their own serial or concurrent queues for executing tasks. Custom queues offer more flexibility and control,

97

making them suitable for scenarios where tasks need to be organized in a specific order or when multiple tasks must run concurrently but isolated from other global system tasks.

Creating Custom Queues

Custom queues are created using the DispatchQueue initializer. You can create either a serial or a concurrent queue:

1. **Serial Queue**: Executes tasks one at a time in the order they are added. This is useful for ensuring that tasks execute in sequence without overlapping.

```swift
Copy code
let serialQueue = DispatchQueue(label: "com.example.serialQueue")

serialQueue.async {
    print("Task 1 running")
}

serialQueue.async {
    print("Task 2 running")
}
```

- **Explanation**: Tasks in a serial queue are executed sequentially, so "Task 1" will complete before "Task 2" starts, regardless of the time taken by each task.

1. **Concurrent Queue**: Executes multiple tasks simultaneously, similar to global queues but with more control over execution behavior.

```swift
Copy code
let concurrentQueue = DispatchQueue(label:
"com.example.concurrentQueue", attributes: .concurrent)

concurrentQueue.async {
    print("Task 1 running")
}

concurrentQueue.async {
    print("Task 2 running concurrently")
}
```

- **Explanation**: Tasks in a concurrent queue can run simultaneously. The order of execution is not guaranteed, and both tasks may complete at the same time or overlap.

When to Use Custom Queues

- **Serial Queues**: When tasks must run in a specific order or when data consistency needs to be maintained, such as writing to a shared resource.
- **Concurrent Queues**: When multiple tasks can be performed simultaneously without interfering with each other, such as processing independent files or parallelizing computations.

Task Management with Executors in Android

In Android, the **Executors** framework provides a versatile and efficient way to manage concurrency. Executors abstract the complexity of thread management, offering a pool of reusable threads for executing tasks in the background. Executors support various models, including single-thread executors, fixed-thread pools, cached-thread pools, and scheduled executors, allowing developers to select the best fit for their application's needs.

1. **SingleThreadExecutor**

99

A **SingleThreadExecutor** uses a single background thread to execute tasks sequentially. It ensures that tasks are executed one after another in a predictable order.

Use Case:

- Suitable for tasks that need to be performed in sequence, such as maintaining a consistent log or processing a series of user inputs that depend on each other.

Example: Using SingleThreadExecutor in Android (Kotlin)

```kotlin
kotlin
Copy code
val executor = Executors.newSingleThreadExecutor()

executor.execute {
    // Perform a background task
    val result = performTask()
    runOnUiThread {
        updateUI(result)
    }
}
```

- **Explanation**: The executor executes tasks sequentially on a single thread. runOnUiThread ensures that the UI update occurs on the main thread after the background task completes.

2. FixedThreadPool

A **FixedThreadPool** creates a pool of a fixed number of threads. It allows multiple tasks to run concurrently, up to the limit of available threads. If more tasks are submitted than available threads, tasks are queued until a thread becomes available.

Use Case:

- Ideal for applications with a predictable number of parallel tasks, such as processing multiple API requests or downloading files concurrently.

Example: Using FixedThreadPool in Android (Kotlin)

```kotlin
Copy code
val executor = Executors.newFixedThreadPool(3)

executor.execute {
    // Task 1: Run in the background
    performTask1()
}

executor.execute {
    // Task 2: Run in the background
    performTask2()
}

executor.execute {
    // Task 3: Run in the background
    performTask3()
}
```

- **Explanation**: The executor maintains a pool of three threads, allowing three tasks to run simultaneously. If a fourth task is submitted, it will wait in the queue until one of the threads is free.

3. CachedThreadPool

A **CachedThreadPool** creates new threads as needed but reuses previously created threads when available. This type of executor has no fixed size and dynamically adjusts based on the number of tasks.

Use Case:

- Suitable for handling short-lived tasks that vary in frequency and duration, such as handling bursts of user requests.

Example: Using CachedThreadPool in Android (Kotlin)

```kotlin
Copy code
val executor = Executors.newCachedThreadPool()

executor.execute {
    // Task 1: Short-lived operation
    performQuickTask()
}

executor.execute {
    // Task 2: Another short-lived operation
    performAnotherTask()
}
```

- **Explanation**: The cached thread pool dynamically creates threads for each task, efficiently handling bursts of operations. If a thread is idle, it is reused for future tasks.

4. ScheduledThreadPool

A **ScheduledThreadPool** supports executing tasks after a delay or at fixed intervals. It is ideal for scheduling recurring tasks, such as periodic data synchronization or maintenance routines.

Use Case:

- Suitable for tasks that need to run periodically, like fetching data from a server at regular intervals.

Example: Using ScheduledThreadPool in Android (Kotlin)

```kotlin
Copy code
val scheduledExecutor = Executors.newScheduledThreadPool(2)
```

```
scheduledExecutor.scheduleAtFixedRate({
    // Perform periodic task
    syncDataWithServer()
}, 0, 1, TimeUnit.HOURS)
```

- **Explanation**: The task syncDataWithServer is scheduled to run every hour with an initial delay of zero. The scheduled executor maintains two threads, which can be used for different scheduled tasks.

5. **Managing Task Lifecycle with ExecutorService**

The ExecutorService interface provides methods for managing the lifecycle of executors and tasks:

1. **Shutting Down Executors**:

- Executors can be shut down gracefully using shutdown(), which stops accepting new tasks but allows already submitted tasks to complete. If immediate shutdown is required, shutdownNow() can be used to attempt to stop all executing and pending tasks.

```kotlin
Copy code
executor.shutdown() // Graceful shutdown
```

1. **Handling Callable Tasks**:

- Unlike Runnable, Callable tasks return a result and can throw exceptions. Using ExecutorService.submit(), developers can handle tasks that produce results using the Future interface.

```kotlin
kotlin
Copy code
val future = executor.submit(Callable {
    performComputation()
})

try {
    val result = future.get() // Blocks until the computation is
    complete
    println("Result: $result")
} catch (e: Exception) {
    e.printStackTrace()
}
```

- **Explanation**: In this example, a Callable task is submitted, and its result is accessed via a Future object, which blocks until the computation completes.

Structuring Asynchronous Code for Scalability

Asynchronous programming is essential for building scalable mobile applications that handle multiple tasks simultaneously while maintaining responsiveness. Proper structuring of asynchronous code ensures that the application can scale efficiently as the complexity and number of tasks grow. This involves leveraging concurrency tools, designing modular code, managing task dependencies, and using best practices for error handling and resource management.

Key Principles for Structuring Asynchronous Code

1. **Modular Design and Task Abstraction**

- Break down complex operations into smaller, independent tasks. This allows for easier management, testing, and reuse of code.
- Use functions, classes, or components (depending on the framework or platform) to encapsulate tasks so that each unit of work can be executed independently or in sequence based on dependencies.

1. **Decouple Task Execution from Task Management**

- Separate the logic for executing tasks from the logic that manages these tasks. This abstraction allows for easy modifications, such as changing the way tasks are scheduled or adding new types of tasks, without impacting the core logic.
- In platforms like iOS, you can use custom queues and operation objects (OperationQueue and Operation classes) for this purpose. In Android, using executors and coroutine scopes can help manage task execution efficiently.

1. **Implement Task Prioritization and Dependency Management**

- Use queues or task managers that support prioritization and dependencies. This ensures that critical tasks are executed first, and tasks that depend on the completion of others are handled appropriately.
- For example, in iOS, **Operation Queues** support dependencies, allowing developers to specify that one task must complete before another starts. In Android, coroutines and WorkManager provide mechanisms for chaining tasks based on dependencies.

1. **Leverage Asynchronous Patterns (Promises, Futures, Async/Await)**

- Patterns like **async/await**, **futures**, and **promises** simplify the structure of asynchronous code, making it easier to read, write, and manage. These patterns allow developers to write asynchronous code in a sequential style, improving readability and maintainability.

- In Android, Kotlin coroutines with suspend functions and async/await are powerful tools for managing asynchronous operations. In iOS, Swift's async/await syntax provides a similar level of abstraction.

1. **Use Lifecycle-Aware Concurrency**

- Tie asynchronous tasks to lifecycle events of UI components, especially in mobile development where activities, view controllers, or fragments have well-defined lifecycles.
- In Android, Kotlin coroutines support lifecycle scopes like viewModelScope and lifecycleScope, ensuring that tasks are canceled when the associated UI component is destroyed, reducing the risk of memory leaks. In iOS, tasks can be managed with reference counting or using tools like Operation objects that are tied to lifecycle events.

1. **Error Handling and Retry Logic**

- Ensure that asynchronous code includes robust error handling and retry logic. Tasks like network requests, which are prone to failures, should be designed to handle exceptions gracefully and retry if necessary, based on predefined conditions.
- Utilize constructs such as try/catch blocks (do/catch in Swift) and structured error handling with coroutines to catch and manage errors effectively.

1. **Scalable Resource Management**

- Limit the number of concurrent tasks based on available resources (e.g., CPU cores, memory). Use thread pools (Android) or custom queues (iOS) to manage the number of concurrent threads.
- Use lightweight constructs like coroutines or GCD tasks that do not consume excessive resources when scaling up the number of tasks.

Case Study: Building a Concurrent Task Manager

This case study illustrates how to build a **Concurrent Task Manager** using scalable asynchronous code principles. The task manager will handle multiple tasks concurrently, manage dependencies, and prioritize tasks efficiently. We'll explore implementations in both iOS (using Swift and GCD/Operation Queues) and Android (using Kotlin and Executors/Coroutines).

Scenario

Imagine an application that needs to perform various background operations, such as:

- Fetching data from multiple APIs.
- Processing large files.
- Synchronizing data periodically.

These tasks need to be managed concurrently but should not overload the system. Certain tasks may depend on the results of others, and some tasks should have higher priority due to their importance to the user experience.

Implementation in iOS (Swift)

The iOS implementation will use **Operation Queues** and **Operations** to structure tasks, manage dependencies, and prioritize execution.

Step 1: Define the Task Class

First, define a custom subclass of Operation that represents a task. This allows us to encapsulate each task's logic and manage dependencies, cancellation, and execution state.

```swift
swift
Copy code
import Foundation

class TaskOperation: Operation {
    private let taskName: String
    private let executionBlock: () -> Void
```

```swift
    init(name: String, block: @escaping () -> Void) {
        self.taskName = name
        self.executionBlock = block
    }

    override func main() {
        if isCancelled {
            return
        }

        print("Executing task: \(taskName)")
        executionBlock()
    }
}
```

- **Explanation**: The TaskOperation class takes a name and a block of code to execute. The main method runs the task, checking if it has been canceled before proceeding.

Step 2: Create the Task Manager

The task manager manages task execution, dependencies, and prioritization using an OperationQueue.

```swift
swift
Copy code
class TaskManager {
    private let operationQueue: OperationQueue

    init() {
        operationQueue = OperationQueue()
        operationQueue.maxConcurrentOperationCount = 4 // Set
        concurrency limit
    }

    func addTask(name: String, block: @escaping () -> Void,
    dependencies: [Operation]? = nil) {
```

```swift
        let task = TaskOperation(name: name, block: block)
        if let dependencies = dependencies {
            for dependency in dependencies {
                task.addDependency(dependency)
            }
        }
        operationQueue.addOperation(task)
    }

    func cancelAllTasks() {
        operationQueue.cancelAllOperations()
    }
}
```

- **Explanation**:
- The TaskManager class encapsulates an OperationQueue that manages the concurrent execution of tasks.
- addTask adds tasks to the queue, optionally setting dependencies.
- The maxConcurrentOperationCount limits the number of tasks running concurrently, ensuring the system is not overloaded.

Step 3: Using the Task Manager

```swift
swift
Copy code
let taskManager = TaskManager()

// Creating sample tasks
taskManager.addTask(name: "Fetch Data") {
    // Simulate network fetch
    print("Fetching data...")
    sleep(2) // Simulate delay
}

taskManager.addTask(name: "Process Data") {
    // Simulate data processing
```

```
    print("Processing data...")
    sleep(3)
}


taskManager.addTask(name: "Sync Data", dependencies: [operation1,
operation2]) {
    // Simulate data synchronization
    print("Syncing data...")
    sleep(2)
}
```

- **Explanation**: Three tasks are created: "Fetch Data," "Process Data," and "Sync Data." The "Sync Data" task depends on the completion of the first two tasks, ensuring they complete before it begins.

Implementation in Android (Kotlin)

The Android implementation uses **Kotlin Coroutines** and **Executors** to manage tasks and dependencies efficiently.

Step 1: Define the Task Function

Each task can be defined as a suspending function using coroutines:

```kotlin
kotlin
Copy code
suspend fun fetchData(): String {
    delay(2000) // Simulate network delay
    println("Data fetched")
    return "Data"
}

suspend fun processData(data: String) {
    delay(3000) // Simulate processing delay
    println("Data processed: $data")
}

suspend fun syncData() {
```

```
    delay(2000) // Simulate sync delay
    println("Data synchronized")
}
```

Step 2: Create the Task Manager Using Coroutines

```kotlin
kotlin
Copy code
import kotlinx.coroutines.*

class TaskManager(private val scope: CoroutineScope) {

    fun executeTasks() {
        scope.launch {
            val data = fetchData()
            processData(data)
            syncData()
        }
    }

    fun cancelAllTasks() {
        scope.cancel() // Cancel all coroutines in the scope
    }
}

// Using the TaskManager
val taskManager = TaskManager(CoroutineScope(Dispatchers.IO))
taskManager.executeTasks()
```

- **Explanation**:
- The TaskManager class uses a CoroutineScope to launch and manage tasks.
- executeTasks runs tasks sequentially, maintaining dependencies between them (e.g., fetching data before processing it).
- The cancelAllTasks method cancels all coroutines running within the scope, ensuring resources are released when the tasks are no longer

needed.

Step 3: Advanced Task Management with WorkManager

For more complex scenarios involving periodic tasks or tasks that must persist even after app restarts, **WorkManager** can be used in Android.

```kotlin
Copy code
val workRequest = OneTimeWorkRequest
Builder<MyWorker>()
    .setConstraints(Constraints.Builder().
setRequiresCharging(true).build())
    .build()

WorkManager.getInstance(context).enqueue(workRequest)
```

- **Explanation**:
- MyWorker is a class that extends Worker and encapsulates the task logic.
- The task is enqueued with constraints (e.g., only execute when charging), ensuring it runs under suitable conditions

Concurrency Patterns and Best Practices

Concurrency patterns help developers structure and manage concurrent tasks in a way that promotes scalability, maintainability, and efficiency. Understanding these patterns and adhering to best practices can greatly enhance the performance and responsiveness of mobile applications, particularly when managing complex interactions and multitasking.

Patterns

1. Producer-Consumer Pattern

The **Producer-Consumer** pattern is used when one or more tasks (producers) generate data or work items and one or more tasks (consumers) process them. This pattern is ideal for managing scenarios where there is a need to balance the workload between producing and consuming resources, such as downloading files and processing them.

Use Case: An image-processing app where images are downloaded (producer) and processed (consumer) asynchronously.

Implementation in iOS (Swift):

```swift
Copy code
```

```
import Foundation

class ImageQueue {
    private var queue = [UIImage]()
    private let queueLock = NSLock()

    func produce(image: UIImage) {
        queueLock.lock()
        queue.append(image)
        queueLock.unlock()
    }

    func consume() -> UIImage? {
        queueLock.lock()
        defer { queueLock.unlock() }
        return queue.isEmpty ? nil : queue.removeFirst()
    }
}
```

- **Explanation**: The ImageQueue class manages the shared resource (an array of images). The producer adds images to the queue, while the consumer retrieves and processes them. The NSLock ensures that only one thread can access the queue at a time, preventing race conditions.

Implementation in Android (Kotlin):

```kotlin
kotlin
Copy code
import java.util.concurrent.BlockingQueue
import java.util.concurrent.LinkedBlockingQueue

val imageQueue: BlockingQueue<Bitmap> = LinkedBlockingQueue()

// Producer coroutine
GlobalScope.launch(Dispatchers.IO) {
    val image = downloadImage() // Simulate image download
```

```
    imageQueue.put(image) // Add image to queue
}

// Consumer coroutine
GlobalScope.launch(Dispatchers.Default) {
    while (true) {
        val image = imageQueue.take() // Retrieve and process image
        processImage(image)
    }
}
```

- **Explanation**: In Android, the BlockingQueue ensures thread-safe operations where producers (downloadImage) add items, and consumers (processImage) take items from the queue concurrently.

2. Singleton Pattern

The **Singleton** pattern ensures that a class has only one instance and provides a global access point to it. This is useful for managing shared resources like database connections, network managers, or configuration objects in mobile apps.

Use Case: A shared network manager to handle API calls throughout the app.

Implementation in iOS (Swift):

```swift
Copy code
class NetworkManager {
    static let shared = NetworkManager()

    private init() {
        // Private initializer to prevent multiple instances
    }

    func fetchData(from url: String) {
```

115

```
    // Perform network request
    }
}
```

```
// Usage
NetworkManager.shared.fetchData(from: "https://api.example.com")
```

- **Explanation**: NetworkManager is a singleton, ensuring that only one instance is ever created. The private init prevents other parts of the code from creating new instances.

Implementation in Android (Kotlin):

```kotlin
Copy code
object NetworkManager {
    fun fetchData(url: String) {
        // Perform network request
    }
}
```

```
// Usage
NetworkManager.fetchData("https://api.example.com")
```

- **Explanation**: The object keyword in Kotlin creates a singleton instance automatically. The NetworkManager object provides a shared instance for making network calls.

3. Observer Pattern

The **Observer** pattern is used for creating a subscription mechanism where objects (observers) subscribe to receive updates or events from another object (subject). This pattern is particularly useful for implementing real-time updates, such as updating UI elements when data changes.

Use Case: An app that listens for changes in network connectivity and updates the UI accordingly.

Implementation in iOS (Swift):

```swift
Copy code
import Foundation

protocol ConnectivityObserver {
    func networkStatusChanged(isConnected: Bool)
}

class ConnectivityManager {
    private var observers = [ConnectivityObserver]()

    func addObserver(_ observer: ConnectivityObserver) {
        observers.append(observer)
    }

    func notifyObservers(isConnected: Bool) {
        for observer in observers {
            observer.networkStatusChanged(isConnected: isConnected)
        }
    }
}

// Usage
class ViewController: UIViewController, ConnectivityObserver {
    func networkStatusChanged(isConnected: Bool) {
        // Update UI based on network status
    }
}
```

- **Explanation**: The ConnectivityManager keeps a list of observers and notifies them when the network status changes. Any class that conforms to the ConnectivityObserver protocol can receive updates.

Implementation in Android (Kotlin):

```kotlin
kotlin
Copy code
interface ConnectivityObserver {
    fun onNetworkStatusChanged(isConnected: Boolean)
}

object ConnectivityManager {
    private val observers = mutableListOf<ConnectivityObserver>()

    fun addObserver(observer: ConnectivityObserver) {
        observers.add(observer)
    }

    fun notifyObservers(isConnected: Boolean) {
        observers.forEach { it.onNetworkStatusChanged(isConnected)
        }
    }
}

// Usage
class MainActivity : AppCompatActivity(), ConnectivityObserver {
    override fun onNetworkStatusChanged(isConnected: Boolean) {
        // Update UI based on network status
    }
}
```

- **Explanation**: ConnectivityManager maintains a list of observers and notifies them of any changes in network connectivity.

Best Practices for UI Updates on the Main Thread

1. **Always Update UI on the Main Thread**:

- In both iOS and Android, UI updates must happen on the main thread to avoid crashes and inconsistencies.
- **Swift Example**: DispatchQueue.main.async { /* Update UI */ }
- **Kotlin Example**: runOnUiThread { /* Update UI */ } or using coroutines

with Dispatchers.Main.

1. **Use Asynchronous Operations for Background Tasks**:

- Offload heavy operations such as network requests or data processing to background threads, and update the UI on the main thread when the task completes.

1. **Leverage Framework-Specific UI Update Mechanisms**:

- In iOS, use OperationQueue with main or DispatchQueue.main.
- In Android, use lifecycle-aware components like LiveData with Observer patterns to update UI based on data changes.

Avoiding Common Pitfalls in Concurrency

1. **Memory Leaks**:

- In iOS, use [weak self] in closures to avoid retaining references, which can lead to memory leaks.
- In Android, use weak references (WeakReference) or lifecycle-aware components (e.g., ViewModel, LiveData) to manage UI updates without leaking memory.

1. **ANR (Application Not Responding) Issues**:

- In Android, blocking the main thread for too long results in ANR errors. Ensure that long-running operations (e.g., network requests, file I/O) are offloaded to background threads using **Executors**, **WorkManager**, or **Kotlin Coroutines**.
- In iOS, avoid blocking the main thread with heavy tasks by using **GCD** or **Operation Queues** for concurrent execution.

1. **Deadlocks and Race Conditions**:

- Use synchronization mechanisms like locks (NSLock in iOS or synchronized blocks in Android) carefully to prevent race conditions but avoid excessive locking that can lead to deadlocks.
- Use higher-level abstractions like coroutines (Kotlin) or operations (Swift) that provide built-in safety mechanisms.

Optimizing Battery and Performance with Efficient Concurrency Usage

1. **Use Background Execution Appropriately**:

- In iOS, leverage background task APIs (e.g., URLSession with background configuration) for long-running operations.
- In Android, use **WorkManager** for deferred or periodic tasks that need to run reliably even if the app is not in the foreground.

1. **Minimize Wake-Ups and Background Processing**:

- Schedule tasks efficiently to avoid frequent wake-ups that drain the battery. Group tasks using WorkManager (Android) or background tasks (iOS) to perform batch operations when the device is idle or charging.

1. **Prioritize Energy Efficiency**:

- Choose appropriate QoS (Quality of Service) levels in iOS (background, utility, etc.) and Dispatchers in Android (e.g., Dispatchers.IO for I/O tasks) to optimize resource usage.
- Avoid using high-priority threads or wake locks unnecessarily, as they can significantly impact battery life.

1. **Test and Monitor Performance**:

- In iOS, use **Instruments** to monitor thread usage, memory allocation, and battery consumption.
- In Android, use the **Android Profiler** to track CPU usage, memory consumption, and network activity. Optimize code based on these insights to reduce battery usage and improve performance.

Networking and Concurrency

Networking and concurrency go hand-in-hand in mobile development, as network requests are often time-consuming operations that must run asynchronously to prevent blocking the user interface (UI). By leveraging asynchronous networking techniques, developers can ensure that their applications remain responsive while efficiently handling data from APIs or other network sources.

Understanding Asynchronous Networking Requests

synchronous networking requests are essential for mobile applications to perform operations such as:

- Fetching data from remote servers (e.g., API calls).
- Downloading or uploading files.
- Synchronizing data in the background.

The core principle is that these network operations should not block the main thread, which is responsible for handling user interactions and updating the UI. By performing these operations asynchronously, the application remains responsive, and the user can interact with the app without experiencing lag or freezes.

How Asynchronous Networking Works

- **Non-Blocking Execution**: Asynchronous requests run independently of the main execution flow. When a request is made, the application continues to run other tasks, and once the request completes, a callback or completion handler is executed to handle the result.
- **Completion Handlers**: These are functions or closures that are called when the network operation completes, either successfully or with an error. They allow the application to react to the result of the request and update the UI or handle errors appropriately.
- **Concurrency Frameworks**: Modern platforms provide concurrency

frameworks such as **URLSession** in iOS and **Retrofit/OkHttp** in Android to manage asynchronous networking efficiently.

Implementing RESTful APIs with Concurrency

RESTful APIs are commonly used in mobile applications to interact with back-end services, retrieve data, authenticate users, and more. Implementing RESTful APIs asynchronously ensures that these operations do not block the main thread.

Key Steps for Implementing RESTful APIs with Concurrency

1. **Define the API Endpoints**:

- Understand the API endpoints, HTTP methods (GET, POST, PUT, DELETE), and expected parameters or headers.
- Use models to structure the data returned by the API, making it easier to parse and manage.

1. **Configure the Network Client**:

- In iOS, use **URLSession** to create and configure network requests.
- In Android, **Retrofit** with **OkHttp** is commonly used for making asynchronous API calls efficiently.

1. **Handle the API Response Asynchronously**:

- Use completion handlers or callbacks to process the response once the request completes.
- Parse the JSON or XML response and update the application state or UI based on the results.

1. **Manage Errors and Retry Logic**:

- Handle errors like network timeouts, server errors (e.g., 500), or client errors (e.g., 404) appropriately.
- Implement retry mechanisms for transient errors such as temporary network outages.

Using URLSession in iOS

URLSession is Apple's framework for performing network operations in iOS. It supports various network tasks, including data requests, file downloads/uploads, and background transfers.

Basic Implementation of URLSession in iOS

1. **Creating a URL and URLRequest**:

```swift
Copy code
let url = URL(string: "https://api.example.com/data")!
var request = URLRequest(url: url)
request.httpMethod = "GET"
request.addValue("application/json", forHTTPHeaderField:
"Content-Type")
```

- **Explanation**: The URL and request are configured for a GET request to fetch data in JSON format from the specified API endpoint.

1. **Creating a Data Task with URLSession**:

```swift
Copy code
let task = URLSession.shared.dataTask(with: request) { data,
response, error in
```

```swift
    guard let data = data, error == nil else {
        print("Error: \(error?.localizedDescription ?? "Unknown
        error")")
        return
    }

    // Process the response data
    do {
        if let json = try JSONSerialization.jsonObject(with: data,
        options: []) as? [String: Any] {
            print("Response JSON: \(json)")
        }
    } catch {
        print("Error parsing JSON: \(error)")
    }
}

// Start the task
task.resume()
```

- **Explanation**:
- dataTask is used to perform the GET request asynchronously.
- A closure is provided to handle the response, parsing the JSON data if the request is successful or logging errors if it fails.
- task.resume() starts the task.

1. **Handling Errors and Retry Mechanisms**:

```swift
swift
Copy code
func fetchDataWithRetry(url: URL, retries: Int = 3) {
    let task = URLSession.shared.dataTask(with: url) { data,
    response, error in
        if let error = error {
```

```
        if retries > 0 {
            print("Retrying... (\(retries) attempts left)")
            fetchDataWithRetry(url: url, retries: retries - 1)
        } else {
            print("Failed after retries:
            \(error.localizedDescription)")
        }
        return
    }

    guard let data = data else { return }
    // Process the response data
  }
  task.resume()
}

fetchDataWithRetry(url: URL(string:
"https://api.example.com/data")!)
```

- **Explanation**:
- The fetchDataWithRetry function tries the request multiple times if it fails, reducing the number of retries with each failure.

Using Retrofit/OkHttp in Android

Retrofit is a popular networking library in Android that works with **OkHttp** to make API calls easier to implement and manage. It supports asynchronous requests using callbacks and integrates well with coroutines.

Basic Implementation of Retrofit in Android

1. **Add Dependencies**:

Add Retrofit and OkHttp dependencies to your build.gradle file:

```gradle
Copy code
implementation 'com.squareup.retrofit2:retrofit:2.9.0'
implementation 'com.squareup.retrofit2:converter-gson:2.9.0'
implementation 'com.squareup.okhttp3:logging-interceptor:4.9.0'
```

1. Define API Endpoints with an Interface:

```kotlin
Copy code
interface ApiService {
    @GET("data")
    suspend fun fetchData(): Response<List<MyDataModel>>
}
```

- **Explanation**: The ApiService interface defines the API call using Retrofit's annotations. The suspend keyword makes it compatible with coroutines.

1. Configure Retrofit Client:

```kotlin
Copy code
val retrofit = Retrofit.Builder()
    .baseUrl("https://api.example.com/")
    .addConverterFactory(GsonConverterFactory.create())
    .client(OkHttpClient.Builder().build())
    .build()

val apiService = retrofit.create(ApiService::class.java)
```

- **Explanation**: Retrofit is configured with the base URL, a converter factory (for JSON parsing), and an OkHttp client.

1. **Making an Asynchronous API Call with Coroutines**:

```kotlin
Copy code
GlobalScope.launch(Dispatchers.IO) {
    try {
        val response = apiService.fetchData()
        if (response.isSuccessful) {
            val data = response.body()
            withContext(Dispatchers.Main) {
                // Update UI with data
            }
        } else {
            println("Error: ${response.code()}")
        }
    } catch (e: Exception) {
        println("Network error: ${e.message}")
    }
}
```

- **Explanation**:
- The network request is made on the IO dispatcher to run in a background thread.
- The response is checked for success, and if valid, the UI is updated using withContext(Dispatchers.Main).

1. **Implementing Error Handling and Retry Mechanisms**:

```kotlin
kotlin
Copy code
suspend fun fetchDataWithRetry(retries: Int = 3):
List<MyDataModel>? {
    var attempts = retries
    while (attempts > 0) {
        try {
            val response = apiService.fetchData()
            if (response.isSuccessful) {
                return response.body()
            }
        } catch (e: Exception) {
            println("Network error: ${e.message}")
        }
        attempts--
        delay(1000) // Optional delay before retrying
    }
    println("Failed after $retries attempts")
    return null
}
```

- **Explanation**: The function retries the network call if it fails, decrementing the number of attempts each time. delay(1000) introduces a pause between retries.

Error Handling and Retry Mechanisms in Network Operations

Handling errors and retrying network requests are critical for maintaining a robust and user-friendly application. Here are some strategies:

1. **Categorizing Errors**:

- **Client Errors (4xx)**: Errors such as 400 (Bad Request) or 404 (Not Found) usually require correcting the request parameters or endpoint.
- **Server Errors (5xx)**: Temporary server issues (e.g., 500 Internal Server Error) may be resolved by retrying after some time.

- **Network Issues**: Errors like timeouts or connectivity problems are transient and can be retried with backoff strategies.

1. **Implementing Retry Logic**:

- **Exponential Backoff**: Increasing the wait time between retries (e.g., doubling it) can reduce the load on the server and improve success rates for transient errors.
- **Retry Limits**: Set a maximum number of retries to prevent infinite loops and conserve resources.

1. **Fallback Mechanisms**:

- Use cached data or a default response when a network request fails, providing the user with a fallback experience rather than displaying an error message immediately.

1. **Logging and Monitoring**:

- Log errors and retry attempts for diagnostics and analytics. Monitoring tools (e.g., Firebase Crashlytics) can provide insights into recurring network issues, helping to optimize the network layer.

Database Operations and Concurrency

Database operations in mobile applications are essential for managing data persistence, retrieval, and updates. However, managing these operations in a concurrent environment poses challenges, especially when ensuring data consistency and performance. This guide will cover managing database operations with concurrency using frameworks like **Core Data** in iOS and **Room** in Android, background operations for data fetching and writing, ensuring data consistency, and building a simple offline-first app.

Managing Database Operations with Concurrency

1. Core Data (iOS)

Core Data is Apple's framework for managing object graphs and data persistence in iOS applications. It supports concurrency, allowing developers to perform background operations while keeping the UI responsive.

Key Components of Core Data Concurrency:

- **Managed Object Context (NSManagedObjectContext)**: This is the primary interface for interacting with Core Data. It represents a single thread of execution for managing and interacting with the object graph.
- **Concurrency Types**:
- **Main Queue Concurrency Type**: Used for UI-related tasks. This

context runs on the main thread.

- **Private Queue Concurrency Type**: Designed for background operations, this context is managed on a separate thread.

Example: Using Core Data with Background Contexts

```swift
Copy code
// Create a private context for background operations
let backgroundContext = NSManagedObjectContext
(concurrencyType: .privateQueueConcurrencyType)
backgroundContext.parent = mainContext
// Set the parent context for merging changes

backgroundContext.perform {
    // Perform background fetch or data operations
    let fetchRequest: NSFetchRequest<MyEntity> =
    MyEntity.fetchRequest()

    do {
        let results = try backgroundContext.fetch(fetchRequest)
        // Process fetched data
    } catch {
        print("Error fetching data: \(error)")
    }
}
```

- **Explanation**: The private context allows for background data fetching. By calling perform, the operations are executed on the appropriate background thread. This ensures that the main context remains free for UI updates.

2. Room (Android)

Room is a persistence library that provides an abstraction layer over SQLite, simplifying database operations in Android applications. Room supports concurrency with its built-in mechanisms for managing background tasks.

Key Components of Room:

- **DAO (Data Access Object)**: Defines methods for accessing the database. DAO methods can be annotated with @Insert, @Update, and @Delete.
- **Database**: The main class that holds the database and serves as the main access point to the underlying SQLite database.
- **Coroutines and LiveData**: Room integrates seamlessly with Kotlin coroutines and LiveData, allowing for asynchronous database operations while keeping the UI responsive.

Example: Using Room with Coroutines

```kotlin
Copy code
@Dao
interface MyDao {
    @Query("SELECT * FROM my_entity")
    suspend fun getAllEntities(): List<MyEntity>

    @Insert
    suspend fun insertEntity(entity: MyEntity)
}

// In a ViewModel
fun fetchData() {
    viewModelScope.launch {
        val entities = myDao.getAllEntities()
// Fetch data in a coroutine
        // Update UI with the retrieved data
    }
}
```

- **Explanation**: The suspend keyword allows DAO methods to be called within a coroutine, enabling non-blocking database operations. The viewModelScope ensures that the coroutine is canceled when the ViewModel is cleared, preventing memory leaks.

Background Thread Operations for Data Fetching and Writing

Managing database operations on background threads is crucial to maintaining app responsiveness. Both Core Data and Room facilitate background operations effectively.

1. **Core Data Background Operations**

Using NSManagedObjectContext with a background queue allows for smooth fetching and saving of data.

Example: Saving Data in Background

```swift
swift
Copy code
let backgroundContext =
NSManagedObjectContext(concurrencyType:
.privateQueueConcurrencyType)
backgroundContext.parent = mainContext

backgroundContext.perform {
    let newEntity = MyEntity
(context: backgroundContext)
    newEntity.name = "New Item"

    do {
        try backgroundContext.save()
        // Save changes to the main context if needed
        try mainContext.save()
    } catch {
        print("Error saving data: \(error)")
    }
}
```

- **Explanation**: New data is added to the background context, which is then saved asynchronously. Changes can also be merged to the main context, ensuring the UI is updated with the latest data.

2. **Room Background Operations**

Room simplifies background operations with coroutines, allowing for fetching and writing tasks to be handled easily.

Example: Writing Data in Background

```kotlin
Copy code
fun insertData(entity: MyEntity) {
    viewModelScope.launch(Dispatchers.IO) {
        myDao.insertEntity(entity)
// Perform insert in background
    }
}
```

- **Explanation**: The Dispatchers.IO context is used to perform database operations in the background. The UI thread remains responsive, while data is inserted asynchronously.

Ensuring Data Consistency and Synchronization

Data consistency is critical when working with concurrent operations. Proper strategies need to be employed to ensure that data remains consistent across different contexts and threads.

1. **Core Data Consistency**

- **Merge Changes**: Use the mergeChanges(from:) method to merge changes from background contexts back to the main context. This keeps data in sync.
- **Save Operations**: Always perform save operations within the appropriate contexts. If using multiple contexts, ensure changes are pushed to the parent context.

Example: Merging Changes in Core Data

```swift
swift
Copy code
NotificationCenter.
default.addObserver(self,
selector: #selector(contextDidSave),
name: NSManagedObjectContext.
didSaveNotification,
object: backgroundContext)

@objc func contextDidSave
(notification: Notification) {
    mainContext.perform {
        self.mainContext.
mergeChanges(from: notification)
    }
}
```

- **Explanation**: Observing the didSaveNotification allows the main context to merge changes from a background context automatically.

2. Room Consistency

- **Transaction Support**: Use transactions when performing multiple database operations to ensure atomicity. If any part of the transaction fails, none of the changes are applied.

Example: Using Transactions in Room

```kotlin
kotlin
Copy code
@Transaction
suspend fun insertEntities(entities: List<MyEntity>) {
    for (entity in entities) {
        insertEntity(entity) // Insert each entity
    }
```

```
}
```

- **Explanation**: The @Transaction annotation ensures that all inserts are treated as a single unit of work, maintaining data integrity.

Building a Simple Offline-First App with Database Concurrency

An offline-first app prioritizes local data storage and availability, ensuring users can access and modify data even without an internet connection. Here's how to build a simple offline-first app with concurrency.

Step 1: Define the Database Model

For Core Data (iOS):

```swift
swift
Copy code
import CoreData

@objc(MyEntity)
class MyEntity: NSManagedObject {
    @NSManaged var name: String?
}
```

For Room (Android):

```kotlin
kotlin
Copy code
@Entity(tableName = "my_entity")
data class MyEntity(
    @PrimaryKey(autoGenerate = true) val id: Int = 0,
    val name: String
)
```

Step 2: Implement the Repository Pattern

The repository pattern abstracts data access, providing a clean API for the rest of the application. It manages local and remote data sources, ensuring data is always available.

iOS Repository Example:

```swift
Copy code
class Repository {
    private let context: NSManagedObjectContext

    init(context: NSManagedObjectContext) {
        self.context = context
    }

    func fetchEntities() -> [MyEntity] {
        // Fetch from Core Data
    }

    func saveEntity(name: String) {
        let entity = MyEntity(context: context)
        entity.name = name
        // Save the context
    }
}
```

Android Repository Example:

```kotlin
Copy code
class Repository(private val myDao: MyDao) {
    val allEntities: LiveData<List<MyEntity>> =
    myDao.getAllEntities()

    suspend fun insert(entity: MyEntity) {
        myDao.insertEntity(entity) // Insert data in the background
    }
}
```

Step 3: Implement Synchronization Logic

When connectivity is available, synchronize local changes with a remote server. Implement a mechanism to fetch data from the server and update the local database accordingly.

iOS Synchronization Example:

```swift
Copy code
func syncDataFromServer() {
    let url = URL(string: "https://api.example.com/data")!
    URLSession.shared.dataTask(with: url) { data, response, error
    in
        // Parse the response and save to Core Data
    }.resume()
}
```

Android Synchronization Example:

```kotlin
Copy code
fun syncData() {
    viewModelScope.launch {
        val remoteData = fetchRemoteData()
        remoteData.forEach { myDao.insertEntity(it) }
    }
}
```

Step 4: Build the User Interface

Create a user interface that allows users to interact with the local database, display data, and sync with remote sources. Ensure UI updates are made on the main thread.

iOS Example:

```swift
Copy code
func displayEntities() {
    let entities = repository.fetchEntities()
    // Update the UI with the fetched entities
```

```
}
```

Android Example:

```kotlin
kotlin
Copy code
class MainActivity : AppCompatActivity() {
    private val repository = Repository(myDao)

    override fun onCreate(savedInstanceState: Bundle?) {
        super.onCreate(savedInstanceState)
        repository.allEntities.observe(this, Observer { entities ->
            // Update UI with the entities
        })
    }
}
```

Concurrency with Multimedia Processing

Multimedia processing, such as video and image handling, requires significant computational resources and can often be time-consuming. To ensure smooth user experiences, especially in applications involving real-time processing like video streaming and image editing, it's crucial to manage these operations asynchronously and efficiently. This guide explores how to leverage concurrency for multimedia processing, focusing on background threading, real-time features, and using platform-specific frameworks like **AVFoundation** in iOS and **CameraX** in Android.

Video and Image Processing on Background Threads

Processing multimedia files (images, videos) is resource-intensive and should always be done on background threads to keep the main thread responsive. Both iOS and Android provide robust frameworks that support background processing.

1. **iOS Example: Image Processing with Background Threads**

In iOS, you can use **GCD** or **OperationQueue** for performing image processing operations on background threads.

Example: Image Processing with GCD

```swift
swift
Copy code
import UIKit

func processImage(_ image: UIImage) {
    DispatchQueue.global(qos: .userInitiated).async {
        // Perform heavy image processing
        let processedImage = self.applyFilter(to: image)

        DispatchQueue.main.async {
            // Update the UI with the processed image
            self.imageView.image = processedImage
        }
    }
}

func applyFilter(to image: UIImage) -> UIImage {
    // Simulate heavy processing
    sleep(2)
    return image // Return processed image
}
```

- **Explanation**: The image processing is performed asynchronously on a background thread, ensuring the UI remains responsive. Once processing is complete, the UI is updated on the main thread.

2. Android Example: Video Processing with Coroutines

In Android, you can leverage Kotlin coroutines to handle multimedia processing seamlessly.

Example: Video Processing in a Coroutine

```kotlin
kotlin
Copy code
import kotlinx.coroutines.*

fun processVideo(videoPath: String) {
```

```
CoroutineScope(Dispatchers.IO).launch {
    val processedVideo = applyVideoFilter(videoPath) //
    Process video in background

    withContext(Dispatchers.Main) {
        // Update UI with the processed video
        updateVideoPlayer(processedVideo)
    }
}
}

suspend fun applyVideoFilter(videoPath: String): String {
    // Simulate heavy processing
    delay(2000)
    return videoPath // Return processed video path
}
```

- **Explanation**: The video processing is done in the IO dispatcher, allowing for concurrent execution without blocking the main thread. After processing, the UI is updated on the main thread.

Leveraging Concurrency for Real-time Multimedia Features

Concurrency is essential for implementing real-time multimedia features, such as live streaming, video editing, and image recognition, where low latency and responsiveness are critical.

1. **Real-time Features in iOS with AVFoundation**

AVFoundation is a powerful framework for working with audiovisual media in iOS. It provides extensive support for capturing, processing, and playing audio and video.

Example: Live Video Capture with AVFoundation

```
swift
Copy code
```

```
import AVFoundation

class VideoCapture: NSObject {
    private var captureSession: AVCaptureSession!

    func startCapture() {
        captureSession = AVCaptureSession()
        guard let videoDevice = AVCaptureDevice.default(for:
        .video) else { return }
        let videoInput = try! AVCaptureDeviceInput(device:
        videoDevice)

        captureSession.addInput(videoInput)

        let videoOutput = AVCaptureVideoDataOutput()
        videoOutput.setSampleBufferDelegate(self, queue:
        DispatchQueue.global(qos: .userInteractive))
        captureSession.addOutput(videoOutput)

        captureSession.startRunning()
    }
}

// Implement AVCaptureVideoDataOutputSampleBufferDelegate methods
for processing frames
```

- **Explanation**: The AVCaptureSession captures live video, and frames are processed in a background thread using a delegate method. This allows for real-time processing of video frames without blocking the UI.

2. Real-time Features in Android with CameraX

CameraX is a Jetpack support library that makes it easier to integrate camera functionalities in Android apps. It provides high-level APIs for capturing photos and videos and processing frames in real-time.

Example: Live Preview with CameraX

```kotlin
Copy code
val cameraProviderFuture =
ProcessCameraProvider.getInstance(context)

cameraProviderFuture.addListener(Runnable {
    val cameraProvider = cameraProviderFuture.get()
    val preview = Preview.Builder().build()
    val cameraSelector = CameraSelector.DEFAULT_BACK_CAMERA

    preview.setSurfaceProvider(viewFinder.surfaceProvider)

    cameraProvider.bindToLifecycle(lifecycleOwner, cameraSelector,
    preview)
}, ContextCompat.getMainExecutor(context))
```

- **Explanation**: The CameraX library sets up a live preview using the device's camera. The bindToLifecycle method automatically manages camera resources based on the lifecycle of the activity or fragment.

Using AVFoundation in iOS and CameraX in Android

Both **AVFoundation** and **CameraX** are designed to simplify multimedia processing and camera functionalities in their respective platforms. They support various operations while efficiently managing concurrency.
AVFoundation (iOS)

- **Video Playback and Processing**: Use AVPlayer for video playback and AVAsset for editing or processing video files.
- **Audio Processing**: Utilize AVAudioEngine for real-time audio processing, allowing effects to be applied dynamically.

Example: Video Playback with AVFoundation

146

```swift
swift
Copy code
import AVKit

class VideoPlayerViewController: UIViewController {
    var player: AVPlayer?

    func playVideo(url: URL) {
        player = AVPlayer(url: url)
        let playerController = AVPlayerViewController()
        playerController.player = player

        DispatchQueue.main.async {
            self.present(playerController, animated: true) {
                self.player?.play()
            }
        }
    }
}
```

- **Explanation**: The AVPlayer plays a video asynchronously, and the UI is updated accordingly.

CameraX (Android)

- **Video Recording**: CameraX supports video recording with easy integration of live previews and image analysis.
- **Image Analysis**: Use ImageAnalysis to process frames in real-time for applications like facial recognition or augmented reality.

Example: Video Recording with CameraX

```kotlin
kotlin
Copy code
```

```
val videoCapture = VideoCapture.Builder().build()

fun startRecording() {
    videoCapture.startRecording(file, executor, object :
    VideoCapture.OnVideoSavedCallback {
        override fun onVideoSaved(outputFileResults:
        OutputFileResults) {
            // Handle successful video save
        }

        override fun onError(videoCaptureError: Int, message:
        String, cause: Throwable?) {
            // Handle error
        }
    })
}
```

- **Explanation**: The VideoCapture class manages video recording, leveraging background threads to handle the recording process.

Implementing Custom Multimedia Operations Using Native Code and Libraries

For specific multimedia processing needs that may not be covered by the built-in frameworks, developers can implement custom operations using native code or third-party libraries.

1. **Using Native Code in iOS (Objective-C/Swift)**

Developers can create custom multimedia processing routines in C or C++ and integrate them with Swift or Objective-C. This is particularly useful for performance-critical applications.

Example: Using C Functions for Image Processing

```
c
Copy code
```

```
// ImageProcessing.h
void applyFilter(unsigned char *imageData, int width, int height);


// ImageProcessing.swift
import Foundation


class ImageProcessor {
    func process(image: UIImage) {
        // Convert UIImage to raw pixel data and call the C
        function
        applyFilter(imageData, width, height)
    }
}
```

- **Explanation**: The applyFilter function is defined in C and can be called from Swift to perform efficient image processing operations.

2. Using Native Libraries in Android

In Android, developers can leverage native libraries (e.g., OpenCV) for image and video processing. JNI (Java Native Interface) can be used to call native code from Kotlin/Java.

Example: Using OpenCV for Image Processing in Android

```kotlin
Copy code
class ImageProcessor {
    init {
        System.loadLibrary("opencv_java4") // Load OpenCV native
        library
    }

    external fun applyFilter(image: Mat): Mat // Native method
    declaration

    fun processImage(bitmap: Bitmap): Bitmap {
        val mat = Mat() // Convert Bitmap to OpenCV Mat
```

```
    val processedMat = applyFilter(mat) // Call native filter
    method
    return Bitmap.createBitmap(processedMat.cols(),
    processedMat.rows(), Bitmap.Config.ARGB_8888)
  }
}
```

- **Explanation**: This example shows how to load a native library and declare a native method for image processing using OpenCV. The processing is done in C/C++, allowing for high-performance operations.

Concurrency in Cross-Platform Development

C ross-platform development enables developers to write applications that run on multiple platforms using a single codebase. Managing concurrency effectively is essential in cross-platform environments, especially for applications that involve intensive data processing, real-time updates, and responsive user interfaces. This guide covers managing concurrency in Flutter and React Native, handling background tasks, and a case study of building a cross-platform app with consistent concurrency implementation.

Managing Concurrency in Flutter

In Flutter, concurrency is managed using **Isolates** and asynchronous programming with **FutureBuilder**. This architecture allows developers to run computations on separate threads without blocking the main thread.

1. **Isolates**

Isolates are independent workers in Dart that run in their own memory space. They do not share memory but can communicate with each other via message passing. This is particularly useful for CPU-bound tasks that could block the main thread if executed synchronously.

Example: Using Isolates for Heavy Computation

151

```dart
Copy code
import 'dart:isolate';

void isolateEntry(SendPort sendPort) {
  // Perform heavy computation
  final result = heavyComputation();
  sendPort.send(result); // Send result back to the main isolate
}

void startIsolate() async {
  final receivePort = ReceivePort();
  await Isolate.spawn(isolateEntry, receivePort.sendPort);

  receivePort.listen((message) {
    print("Received result: $message");
  });
}

int heavyComputation() {
  // Simulate heavy computation
  return 42; // Example result
}
```

- **Explanation**: The isolateEntry function performs heavy computation in a separate isolate. The result is sent back to the main isolate using a SendPort, allowing the UI to remain responsive.

2. FutureBuilder

The FutureBuilder widget in Flutter is used to build widgets based on the state of a Future. It allows developers to handle asynchronous operations easily and update the UI based on the completion of those operations.

Example: Using FutureBuilder for Asynchronous Data Fetching

```dart
dart
Copy code
Future<String> fetchData() async {
  await Future.delayed(Duration(seconds: 2)); // Simulate network
  delay
  return "Data fetched";
}

class MyWidget extends StatelessWidget {
  @override
  Widget build(BuildContext context) {
    return FutureBuilder<String>(
      future: fetchData(),
      builder: (context, snapshot) {
        if (snapshot.connectionState == ConnectionState.waiting) {
          return CircularProgressIndicator(); // Show loading
          indicator
        } else if (snapshot.hasError) {
          return Text("Error: ${snapshot.error}");
        } else {
          return Text("Result: ${snapshot.data}"); // Display
          fetched data
        }
      },
    );
  }
}
```

- **Explanation**: The FutureBuilder listens to the Future returned by fetchData(). It shows a loading indicator while waiting for the data, handles errors, and displays the fetched data once available.

Concurrency Techniques in React Native

In React Native, concurrency is managed primarily through the JavaScript concurrency model, which relies on the event loop, Promises, and the use of native modules for heavy tasks.

1. JavaScript Concurrency Model

JavaScript uses a single-threaded event loop to handle concurrency. This means that while JavaScript itself is single-threaded, it can handle asynchronous operations through callbacks, Promises, and async/await syntax. The key is to avoid blocking the main thread, particularly for long-running tasks.

Example: Using Promises and Async/Await

```javascript
Copy code
async function fetchData() {
    try {
        const response = await
        fetch('https://api.example.com/data');
        const data = await response.json();
        console.log('Fetched data:', data);
    } catch (error) {
        console.error('Error fetching data:', error);
    }
}

// Call the async function
fetchData();
```

- **Explanation**: The fetchData function uses async/await to perform a network request asynchronously, allowing other operations to run without blocking the main thread.

2. Native Modules

For CPU-intensive operations that might block the JavaScript thread, React Native allows developers to create native modules. These modules run in separate threads and can be used to perform heavy computations or access device features directly.

Example: Creating a Native Module

In **Java** (Android):

```java
java
Copy code
public class MyNativeModule extends ReactContextBaseJavaModule {
    public MyNativeModule(ReactApplicationContext reactContext) {
        super(reactContext);
    }

    @ReactMethod
    public void heavyComputation(Promise promise) {
        // Perform heavy computation in a separate thread
        new Thread(() -> {
            int result = performComputation();
            promise.resolve(result);
        }).start();
    }

    private int performComputation() {
        // Simulate heavy computation
        return 42;
    }

    @Override
    public String getName() {
        return "MyNativeModule";
    }
}
```

In JavaScript:

```javascript
javascript
Copy code
import { NativeModules } from 'react-native';

const { MyNativeModule } = NativeModules;

MyNativeModule.heavyComputation()
    .then(result => {
        console.log('Result from native module:', result);
```

```
  })
  .catch(error => {
      console.error('Error:', error);
  });
```

- **Explanation**: The native module performs heavy computations on a separate thread and sends the result back to JavaScript using Promises.

Handling Background Tasks Across Platforms

Managing background tasks efficiently is crucial for both platforms, especially for tasks like data syncing, notifications, or background processing.

1. **Background Tasks in Flutter**

Flutter supports background execution using plugins like **workmanager** or **flutter_background** for scheduling background tasks, especially for tasks that need to run even when the app is not active.

Example: Using WorkManager Plugin

```dart
dart
Copy code
import 'package:workmanager/workmanager.dart';

void callbackDispatcher() {
  Workmanager().executeTask((task, inputData) {
    // Perform background task
    return Future.value(true);
  });
}

// Initialize WorkManager
void main() {
  Workmanager().initialize(
    callbackDispatcher,
    isInDebugMode: true,
```

```
  );
  Workmanager().registerPeriodicTask(
    "1",
    "simplePeriodicTask",
    frequency: Duration(minutes: 15),
  );
}
```

- **Explanation**: The callbackDispatcher function handles background tasks, and the registerPeriodicTask schedules the task to run periodically.

2. Background Tasks in React Native

In React Native, libraries like **react-native-background-fetch** and **react-native-background-task** can be used to handle background tasks.

Example: Using react-native-background-fetch

```javascript
Copy code
import BackgroundFetch from 'react-native-background-fetch';

const onFetch = async (taskId) => {
    console.log('[BackgroundFetch] taskId:', taskId);
    // Perform background fetch operation
    // Call finish when done
    BackgroundFetch.finish(taskId);
};

// Initialize background fetch
BackgroundFetch.configure({
    minimumFetchInterval: 15, // Fetch every 15 minutes
}, onFetch);
```

- **Explanation**: This setup configures the background fetch with a minimum interval and defines a function that runs when the task is triggered.

Case Study: Building a Cross-Platform App with Consistent Concurrency Implementation

Scenario: Suppose you are building a cross-platform app that requires real-time data syncing, video processing, and image handling. The app should work seamlessly on both iOS and Android while providing a consistent user experience.

Step 1: Defining the Core Features

- **Real-Time Sync**: Sync user data and preferences with a remote server.
- **Multimedia Processing**: Allow users to upload and process images and videos.
- **Background Tasks**: Fetch data and handle multimedia operations in the background.

Step 2: Implementing Concurrency in Flutter

1. **Real-Time Sync with Isolates**:

- Use isolates to manage data sync operations without blocking the UI. Use a Stream to listen for updates and notify the UI.

1. **Image and Video Processing**:

- Leverage packages like image or video_player in combination with isolates for processing tasks.

1. **Background Tasks**:

- Use the **workmanager** plugin to schedule data fetch and processing tasks in the background.

Step 3: Implementing Concurrency in React Native

1. **Real-Time Sync with Promises**:

- Use async/await to manage real-time sync operations with the server, updating the UI based on data fetched.

1. **Image and Video Processing**:

- Utilize native modules to handle image processing tasks in separate threads, ensuring that heavy computations don't block the UI.

1. **Background Tasks**:

- Implement background fetch using **react-native-background-fetch** to manage periodic syncs or data fetching.

Concurrency in Cross-Platform Development

C ross-platform development enables developers to write applications that run on multiple platforms using a single codebase. Managing concurrency effectively is essential in cross-platform environments, especially for applications that involve intensive data processing, real-time updates, and responsive user interfaces. This guide covers managing concurrency in Flutter and React Native, handling background tasks, and a case study of building a cross-platform app with consistent concurrency implementation.

Managing Concurrency in Flutter

In Flutter, concurrency is managed using **Isolates** and asynchronous programming with **FutureBuilder**. This architecture allows developers to run computations on separate threads without blocking the main thread.

1. Isolates

Isolates are independent workers in Dart that run in their own memory space. They do not share memory but can communicate with each other via message passing. This is particularly useful for CPU-bound tasks that could block the main thread if executed synchronously.

Example: Using Isolates for Heavy Computation

```dart
Copy code
import 'dart:isolate';

void isolateEntry(SendPort sendPort) {
  // Perform heavy computation
  final result = heavyComputation();
  sendPort.send(result); // Send result back to the main isolate
}

void startIsolate() async {
  final receivePort = ReceivePort();
  await Isolate.spawn(isolateEntry, receivePort.sendPort);

  receivePort.listen((message) {
    print("Received result: $message");
  });
}

int heavyComputation() {
  // Simulate heavy computation
  return 42; // Example result
}
```

- **Explanation**: The isolateEntry function performs heavy computation in a separate isolate. The result is sent back to the main isolate using a SendPort, allowing the UI to remain responsive.

2. FutureBuilder

The FutureBuilder widget in Flutter is used to build widgets based on the state of a Future. It allows developers to handle asynchronous operations easily and update the UI based on the completion of those operations.

Example: Using FutureBuilder for Asynchronous Data Fetching

```dart
Copy code
Future<String> fetchData() async {
  await Future.delayed(Duration(seconds: 2)); // Simulate network
  delay
  return "Data fetched";
}

class MyWidget extends StatelessWidget {
  @override
  Widget build(BuildContext context) {
    return FutureBuilder<String>(
      future: fetchData(),
      builder: (context, snapshot) {
        if (snapshot.connectionState == ConnectionState.waiting) {
          return CircularProgressIndicator(); // Show loading
          indicator
        } else if (snapshot.hasError) {
          return Text("Error: ${snapshot.error}");
        } else {
          return Text("Result: ${snapshot.data}"); // Display
          fetched data
        }
      },
    );
  }
}
```

- **Explanation**: The FutureBuilder listens to the Future returned by fetchData(). It shows a loading indicator while waiting for the data, handles errors, and displays the fetched data once available.

Concurrency Techniques in React Native

In React Native, concurrency is managed primarily through the JavaScript concurrency model, which relies on the event loop, Promises, and the use of native modules for heavy tasks.

1. JavaScript Concurrency Model

JavaScript uses a single-threaded event loop to handle concurrency. This means that while JavaScript itself is single-threaded, it can handle asynchronous operations through callbacks, Promises, and async/await syntax. The key is to avoid blocking the main thread, particularly for long-running tasks.

Example: Using Promises and Async/Await

```javascript
Copy code
async function fetchData() {
    try {
        const response = await
        fetch('https://api.example.com/data');
        const data = await response.json();
        console.log('Fetched data:', data);
    } catch (error) {
        console.error('Error fetching data:', error);
    }
}

// Call the async function
fetchData();
```

- **Explanation**: The fetchData function uses async/await to perform a network request asynchronously, allowing other operations to run without blocking the main thread.

2. Native Modules

For CPU-intensive operations that might block the JavaScript thread, React Native allows developers to create native modules. These modules run in separate threads and can be used to perform heavy computations or access device features directly.

Example: Creating a Native Module

In **Java** (Android):

163

```java
java
Copy code
public class MyNativeModule extends ReactContextBaseJavaModule {
    public MyNativeModule(ReactApplicationContext reactContext) {
        super(reactContext);
    }

    @ReactMethod
    public void heavyComputation(Promise promise) {
        // Perform heavy computation in a separate thread
        new Thread(() -> {
            int result = performComputation();
            promise.resolve(result);
        }).start();
    }

    private int performComputation() {
        // Simulate heavy computation
        return 42;
    }

    @Override
    public String getName() {
        return "MyNativeModule";
    }
}
```

In **JavaScript**:

```javascript
javascript
Copy code
import { NativeModules } from 'react-native';

const { MyNativeModule } = NativeModules;

MyNativeModule.heavyComputation()
    .then(result => {
        console.log('Result from native module:', result);
```

```
})
.catch(error => {
    console.error('Error:', error);
});
```

- **Explanation**: The native module performs heavy computations on a separate thread and sends the result back to JavaScript using Promises.

Handling Background Tasks Across Platforms

Managing background tasks efficiently is crucial for both platforms, especially for tasks like data syncing, notifications, or background processing.

1. **Background Tasks in Flutter**

Flutter supports background execution using plugins like **workmanager** or **flutter_background** for scheduling background tasks, especially for tasks that need to run even when the app is not active.

Example: Using WorkManager Plugin

```dart
dart
Copy code
import 'package:workmanager/workmanager.dart';

void callbackDispatcher() {
  Workmanager().executeTask((task, inputData) {
    // Perform background task
    return Future.value(true);
  });
}

// Initialize WorkManager
void main() {
  Workmanager().initialize(
    callbackDispatcher,
    isInDebugMode: true,
```

```
  );
  Workmanager().registerPeriodicTask(
    "1",
    "simplePeriodicTask",
    frequency: Duration(minutes: 15),
  );
}
```

- **Explanation**: The callbackDispatcher function handles background tasks, and the registerPeriodicTask schedules the task to run periodically.

2. Background Tasks in React Native

In React Native, libraries like **react-native-background-fetch** and **react-native-background-task** can be used to handle background tasks.

Example: Using react-native-background-fetch

```javascript
javascript
Copy code
import BackgroundFetch from 'react-native-background-fetch';

const onFetch = async (taskId) => {
    console.log('[BackgroundFetch] taskId:', taskId);
    // Perform background fetch operation
    // Call finish when done
    BackgroundFetch.finish(taskId);
};

// Initialize background fetch
BackgroundFetch.configure({
    minimumFetchInterval: 15, // Fetch every 15 minutes
}, onFetch);
```

- **Explanation**: This setup configures the background fetch with a minimum interval and defines a function that runs when the task is triggered.

Case Study: Building a Cross-Platform App with Consistent Concurrency Implementation

Scenario: Suppose you are building a cross-platform app that requires real-time data syncing, video processing, and image handling. The app should work seamlessly on both iOS and Android while providing a consistent user experience.

Step 1: Defining the Core Features

- **Real-Time Sync**: Sync user data and preferences with a remote server.
- **Multimedia Processing**: Allow users to upload and process images and videos.
- **Background Tasks**: Fetch data and handle multimedia operations in the background.

Step 2: Implementing Concurrency in Flutter

1. **Real-Time Sync with Isolates**:

- Use isolates to manage data sync operations without blocking the UI. Use a Stream to listen for updates and notify the UI.

1. **Image and Video Processing**:

- Leverage packages like image or video_player in combination with isolates for processing tasks.

1. **Background Tasks**:

- Use the **workmanager** plugin to schedule data fetch and processing tasks in the background.

Step 3: Implementing Concurrency in React Native

1. **Real-Time Sync with Promises**:

- Use async/await to manage real-time sync operations with the server, updating the UI based on data fetched.

1. **Image and Video Processing**:

- Utilize native modules to handle image processing tasks in separate threads, ensuring that heavy computations don't block the UI.

1. **Background Tasks**:

- Implement background fetch using **react-native-background-fetch** to manage periodic syncs or data fetching.

Advanced Concurrency Techniques

As applications grow in complexity, so does the need for sophisticated concurrency techniques that allow developers to manage tasks efficiently, ensure responsiveness, and maintain data integrity. This guide will explore advanced concurrency patterns, structured concurrency, building custom concurrency APIs, and best practices for thread synchronization and resource locking.

Advanced Patterns

1. Promise/Future

Promises and **Futures** are constructs that represent a value that may be available now, or in the future, or never. They are commonly used to handle asynchronous operations and provide a cleaner way to manage callbacks compared to traditional methods.

- **Promise**: An object that represents the eventual completion (or failure) of an asynchronous operation and its resulting value.
- **Future**: A placeholder for a result that is initially unknown but will be resolved in the future.

Example in JavaScript (Promise):

```javascript
javascript
Copy code
function fetchData() {
    return new Promise((resolve, reject) => {
        setTimeout(() => {
            const data = "Data fetched";
            resolve(data); // Resolving the promise with the
            fetched data
        }, 2000);
    });
}

fetchData()
    .then(result => {
        console.log(result);
    })
    .catch(error => {
        console.error("Error:", error);
    });
```

Example in Swift (Future):

```swift
swift
Copy code
import Foundation

func fetchData() -> Future<String, Error> {
    return Future { promise in
        DispatchQueue.global().async {
            sleep(2) // Simulate network delay
            promise(.success("Data fetched")) // Complete the
            future with a value
        }
    }
}

fetchData()
    .sink(receiveCompletion: { completion in
```

```
    print("Completion: \(completion)")
}, receiveValue: { value in
    print("Value: \(value)")
})
```

2. Async/Await

Async/Await is a syntactic feature that simplifies asynchronous programming by allowing developers to write asynchronous code in a sequential manner. This pattern is available in many modern programming languages, including JavaScript, Swift, and Kotlin.

Example in JavaScript:

```javascript
Copy code
async function fetchData() {
    try {
        const response = await
        fetch('https://api.example.com/data');
        const data = await response.json();
        console.log(data);
    } catch (error) {
        console.error('Error:', error);
    }
}

fetchData();
```

Example in Swift:

```swift
Copy code
func fetchData() async throws -> String {
    let (data, response) = try await URLSession.shared.data(from:
    URL(string: "https://api.example.com/data")!)
    return String(data: data, encoding: .utf8) ?? "No data"
}
```

```
Task {
    do {
        let result = try await fetchData()
        print(result)
    } catch {
        print("Error:", error)
    }
}
```

Example in Kotlin:

```kotlin
kotlin
Copy code
import kotlinx.coroutines.*

suspend fun fetchData(): String {
    delay(2000) // Simulate network delay
    return "Data fetched"
}

fun main() {
    runBlocking {
        try {
            val result = fetchData()
            println(result)
        } catch (e: Exception) {
            println("Error: ${e.message}")
        }
    }
}
```

3. RxJava/RxSwift

RxJava and **RxSwift** are reactive programming libraries that allow developers to work with asynchronous data streams using observable sequences. They simplify the handling of asynchronous events and enable elegant composition of operations.

Example in RxJava:

```java
java
Copy code
Observable.fromCallable(() -> {
    // Simulate fetching data
    Thread.sleep(2000);
    return "Data fetched";
})
.subscribeOn(Schedulers.io())
.observeOn(AndroidSchedulers.mainThread())
.subscribe(result -> {
    System.out.println(result);
}, throwable -> {
    System.err.println("Error: " + throwable);
});
```

Example in RxSwift:

```swift
swift
Copy code
let observable = Observable<String>.create { observer in
    // Simulate fetching data
    DispatchQueue.global().async {
        sleep(2)
        observer.onNext("Data fetched")
        observer.onCompleted()
    }
    return Disposables.create()
}

observable
    .observeOn(MainScheduler.instance)
    .subscribe(onNext: { data in
        print(data)
    }, onError: { error in
        print("Error:", error)
    })
    .disposed(by: disposeBag)
```

Structured Concurrency in Kotlin and Swift

Structured concurrency is a programming paradigm that simplifies asynchronous programming by enforcing a structured approach to concurrency. It ensures that all coroutines (in Kotlin) or asynchronous tasks (in Swift) are bound to a specific scope and lifetime, making it easier to manage cancellations and exceptions.

1. Structured Concurrency in Kotlin

Kotlin's coroutines support structured concurrency through the use of CoroutineScope and structured functions like launch and async.

Example:

```kotlin
kotlin
Copy code
fun main() = runBlocking {
    // This is the coroutine scope
    launch {
        // Coroutine launched in the scope
        delay(1000)
        println("Task from coroutine")
    }
    println("Coroutine scope is running")
}
```

- **Explanation**: The runBlocking function provides a coroutine scope that keeps the main thread alive until all coroutines in the scope complete.

2. Structured Concurrency in Swift

Swift also embraces structured concurrency with the introduction of async/await in Swift 5.5. It provides a clean and structured way to manage asynchronous tasks.

Example:

```swift
Copy code
func fetchData() async {
    let data = await withTaskGroup(of: String.self) { group in
        group.addTask {
            // Simulate fetching data
            return "Fetched data"
        }
        return await group.reduce("", +) // Combine results
    }
    print(data)
}

Task {
    await fetchData()
}
```

- **Explanation**: The withTaskGroup allows the creation of a group of tasks that can run concurrently, and await waits for the completion of those tasks in a structured manner.

Building Custom Concurrency APIs

Creating custom concurrency APIs allows developers to encapsulate concurrency logic and provide a consistent interface for task management. This can be particularly useful when specific functionality is needed that is not covered by existing libraries.

Example: Custom Concurrency API in Swift

```swift
Copy code
class CustomConcurrencyManager {
    private let queue = DispatchQueue(label:
    "com.example.customQueue")
```

```
    func performTaskAsync(task: @escaping () -> Void) {
        queue.async {
            task()
        }
    }

    func performTaskWithCompletion(task: @escaping () -> Void,
    completion: @escaping () -> Void) {
        queue.async {
            task()
            DispatchQueue.main.async {
                completion()
            }
        }
    }
}

// Usage
let manager = CustomConcurrencyManager()
manager.performTaskAsync {
    // Perform a background task
    print("Task running in background")
}

manager.performTaskWithCompletion(task: {
    // Perform another task
    print("Another task running")
}, completion: {
    print("Task completed, now back to main thread")
})
```

- **Explanation**: This custom concurrency manager allows tasks to be executed asynchronously on a dedicated queue, with an option to execute a completion handler on the main thread.

Best Practices for Thread Synchronization and Resource Locking

When dealing with concurrency, ensuring that data integrity is maintained while multiple threads or processes are accessing shared resources is crucial. Here are best practices for synchronization and resource locking:

1. **Use Appropriate Synchronization Mechanisms**:

- Use high-level constructs such as DispatchQueue in Swift and synchronized blocks or ReentrantLock in Kotlin to manage access to shared resources.
- Prefer using immutable objects where possible, as they are inherently thread-safe.

1. **Minimize Locking**:

- Keep the scope of locks as small as possible to reduce contention and improve performance. Avoid long-held locks that can lead to bottlenecks.

1. **Avoid Nested Locks**:

- Nested locks can lead to deadlocks. If multiple threads try to acquire multiple locks at the same time, it can create a situation where each thread is waiting for a lock held by another, causing the application to hang.

1. **Use Read-Write Locks**:

- If your application frequently reads shared data but rarely writes to it, consider using read-write locks, which allow multiple readers but exclusive access for writers.

1. **Test for Race Conditions**:

- Implement comprehensive testing to identify and fix race conditions, particularly in critical sections of the code where shared resources are accessed.

1. **Leverage High-Level Abstractions**:

- Use high-level concurrency libraries and frameworks that manage synchronization internally. For instance, Kotlin coroutines and Swift's structured concurrency provide safe ways to handle concurrent operations without manual locking.

1. **Implement Timeout Mechanisms**:

- When acquiring locks, consider implementing timeout mechanisms to prevent threads from waiting indefinitely

Testing and Debugging Concurrency in Mobile Apps

T esting and debugging concurrent code in mobile applications are critical tasks that help ensure reliability, performance, and a smooth user experience. Given the complexities introduced by multithreading and asynchronous operations, developers must employ specific strategies and tools for effective testing and debugging.

Testing Asynchronous Code in iOS and Android

Testing asynchronous code can be challenging, but it's essential for ensuring that tasks execute correctly and that the application behaves as expected in concurrent scenarios. Both iOS and Android provide tools and frameworks for testing asynchronous operations.

1. Testing Asynchronous Code in iOS

In iOS, XCTest framework allows for unit testing asynchronous code by using expectations to wait for asynchronous operations to complete.

Example: Testing Asynchronous Code in Swift

```swift
swift
Copy code
import XCTest

class MyTests: XCTestCase {
    func testFetchData() {
        let expectation = self.expectation(description: "Data
        fetched")

        fetchData { data in
            XCTAssertNotNil(data, "Data should not be nil")
            expectation.fulfill() // Signal that the async task is
            complete
        }

        waitForExpectations(timeout: 5, handler: nil) // Wait for
        expectations
    }
}
```

- **Explanation**: An expectation is created to wait for the completion of an asynchronous task. The test will wait until expectation.fulfill() is called, ensuring that the asynchronous operation has completed before making assertions.

2. Testing Asynchronous Code in Android

In Android, JUnit along with the LiveData and coroutines support testing asynchronous code. You can use runBlockingTest for testing coroutines, which allows you to control the execution of coroutines.

Example: Testing Asynchronous Code in Kotlin

```kotlin
kotlin
Copy code
import androidx.arch.core.executor.testing.InstantTaskExecutorRule
import kotlinx.coroutines.test.runBlockingTest
```

```
import org.junit.Rule
import org.junit.Test

class MyViewModelTest {
    @get:Rule
    var instantExecutorRule = InstantTaskExecutorRule() // Ensure
    LiveData updates are executed synchronously

    @Test
    fun testFetchData() = runBlockingTest {
        val viewModel = MyViewModel()
        viewModel.fetchData()

        // Observe LiveData and assert data is not null
        viewModel.data.observeForever {
            assertNotNull(it)
        }
    }
}
```

- **Explanation**: The InstantTaskExecutorRule ensures that LiveData updates occur immediately, making it easier to test asynchronous data fetching.

Debugging Multithreaded Apps: Tools and Techniques

Debugging multithreaded applications can be complex due to the non-deterministic nature of concurrency. Here are tools and techniques for effectively debugging such applications:
1. **Debugging Tools in iOS**

- **Xcode Debugger**: Xcode provides a robust debugger that allows you to inspect thread states, view variables, and set breakpoints. You can step through code and watch how different threads interact.
- **Instruments**: Instruments is a powerful performance analysis and

profiling tool. It can be used to analyze memory usage, CPU usage, and thread activity, helping to identify issues like deadlocks and race conditions.

2. Debugging Tools in Android

- **Android Studio Debugger**: Android Studio's debugger lets you inspect threads, evaluate expressions, and monitor variable values during execution. You can pause the app at breakpoints to inspect the current state of each thread.
- **StrictMode**: This tool helps catch accidental disk or network access on the main thread. Enabling StrictMode can help developers identify potential performance bottlenecks.

Simulating Network Delays and Background Task Failures

Testing how an app behaves under adverse conditions, such as network delays or background task failures, is crucial for ensuring robustness.

1. Simulating Network Delays in iOS

You can use URL Protocols to simulate network delays in your tests.

Example: Simulating Network Delays

```swift
Copy code
class MockURLProtocol: URLProtocol {
    override class func canInit(with request: URLRequest) -> Bool {
        return true
    }

    override class func canonicalRequest(for request: URLRequest)
    -> URLRequest {
        return request
    }

    override func startLoading() {
```

```
    // Simulate network delay
    DispatchQueue.global().asyncAfter(deadline: .now() + 2) {
        let response = HTTPURLResponse(url: self.request.url!,
        statusCode: 200, httpVersion: nil, headerFields: nil)
        self.client?.urlProtocol(self, didReceive: response!,
        cacheStoragePolicy: .notAllowed)
        self.client?.urlProtocol(self, didLoad: Data("Mock
        data".utf8))
        self.client?.urlProtocolDidFinishLoading(self)
    }
    }

    override func stopLoading() {}
}

// In your test
let config = URLSessionConfiguration.default
config.protocolClasses = [MockURLProtocol.self]
let session = URLSession(configuration: config)
```

2. Simulating Network Delays in Android

In Android, you can use libraries like **Mockito** to mock network calls and simulate delays.

Example: Simulating Network Delays

```kotlin
Copy code
val mockApiService = mock(ApiService::class.java)
whenever(mockApiService.fetchData()).thenAnswer {
    Thread.sleep(2000) // Simulate delay
    return@thenAnswer Response.success("Mock data")
}
```

183

Handling Background Task Failures

Testing how the app reacts to background task failures is crucial for maintaining user experience.

1. Simulating Failures in iOS

You can simulate failures in your mocked network requests by throwing errors.

```swift
swift
Copy code
class MockURLProtocol: URLProtocol {
    // Same setup as before...
    override func startLoading() {
        // Simulate failure
        DispatchQueue.global().asyncAfter(deadline: .now() + 1) {
            let error = NSError(domain: "NetworkError", code: 404,
            userInfo: nil)
            self.client?.urlProtocol(self, didFailWithError: error)
        }
    }
}
```

2. Simulating Failures in Android

Using **Mockito,** you can also simulate errors returned from your API service.

```kotlin
kotlin
Copy code
whenever(mockApiService.fetchData()).thenThrow(RuntimeException("Network
Error"))
```

Automated Testing for Concurrency Scenarios

Automated testing is critical for ensuring the reliability of concurrent code. Here's how to implement automated testing for concurrency scenarios effectively.

1. **Automated Testing in iOS**

You can use XCTest for writing unit tests that check the correctness of concurrent operations.

Example: Testing for Concurrency Issues

```swift
Copy code
func testConcurrentAccess() {
    let expectation = self.expectation(description: "Concurrent
    Access")
    let queue = DispatchQueue(label: "com.test.concurrent",
    attributes: .concurrent)

    let group = DispatchGroup()

    for _ in 0..<100 {
        group.enter()
        queue.async {
            // Simulate some work
            self.repository.fetchData()
            group.leave()
        }
    }

    group.notify(queue: DispatchQueue.main) {
        expectation.fulfill()
    }

    waitForExpectations(timeout: 5, handler: nil)
}
```

- **Explanation**: This test simulates concurrent access to a repository, ensuring that the fetchData method can handle multiple concurrent calls correctly.

2. **Automated Testing in Android**

In Android, you can use JUnit and coroutines to write tests that simulate

185

concurrency.

Example: Testing Concurrency with Coroutines

```kotlin
kotlin
Copy code
@Test
fun testConcurrentFetchData() = runBlockingTest {
    val jobs = List(100) {
        launch {
            repository.fetchData() // Fetch data concurrently
        }
    }
    jobs.forEach { it.join() } // Wait for all coroutines to
    complete
    // Assertions to validate state
}
```

- **Explanation**: This test launches multiple coroutines that call fetchData concurrently, ensuring the method handles concurrent requests without errors.

Performance Optimization and Concurrency

Optimizing the performance of mobile applications is essential for providing users with a smooth and responsive experience. Performance issues, particularly those related to concurrency, can lead to sluggishness, high memory usage, and poor user engagement. This guide covers profiling tools for iOS and Android, techniques for detecting and fixing performance bottlenecks, methods for minimizing memory usage, and a case study demonstrating performance optimization in a real-world application.

Profiling Tools for iOS and Android

Profiling tools allow developers to analyze their applications' performance, identify bottlenecks, and optimize resource usage effectively.

1. Profiling Tools for iOS (Instruments)

Instruments is a powerful performance analysis and profiling tool bundled with Xcode. It provides various templates to profile different aspects of an application, including CPU usage, memory allocation, network activity, and more.

Key Instruments for Profiling:

- **Time Profiler**: Measures the CPU usage and helps identify functions that consume significant processing time.
- **Allocations**: Tracks memory usage and object allocation, allowing developers to identify memory leaks and excessive memory consumption.
- **Activity Monitor**: Displays real-time statistics about the app's resource usage, including CPU and memory consumption.
- **Network**: Monitors network activity to analyze requests, data received, and overall network performance.

Example Usage:

1. Open Instruments from Xcode.
2. Select a profiling template (e.g., Time Profiler).
3. Run your app and interact with it to simulate real usage.
4. Analyze the recorded data to identify performance bottlenecks.

2. Profiling Tools for Android (Android Profiler)

Android Profiler is integrated into Android Studio and provides a suite of tools for monitoring an app's performance in real-time.

Key Profiling Features:

- **CPU Profiler**: Visualizes CPU activity, showing which threads are running and what methods are consuming the most CPU time.
- **Memory Profiler**: Tracks memory allocation, allowing developers to identify leaks and memory consumption patterns.
- **Network Profiler**: Monitors network requests, showing request/response times and data transfer details.

Example Usage:

1. Open Android Studio and launch the app in debug mode.
2. Navigate to the Profiler tab.
3. Select the relevant profiler (CPU, Memory, Network) and interact with

the app to gather data.

4. Analyze the recorded data to pinpoint performance issues.

Detecting and Fixing Performance Bottlenecks

Detecting and fixing performance bottlenecks is critical for ensuring smooth app performance. Here are common strategies for identifying and resolving issues:

1. **Identifying Bottlenecks**

- **Analyze CPU Usage**: Use profiling tools to check which methods consume the most CPU resources. Look for long-running tasks, especially those running on the main thread.
- **Monitor Memory Usage**: Identify memory spikes or leaks that could affect performance. High memory consumption can lead to increased garbage collection or even crashes.
- **Profile Network Activity**: Check network latency and data transfer times. Poor network performance can lead to slow data fetching and affect the user experience.

2. **Fixing Bottlenecks**

- **Optimize Algorithms**: Review and optimize algorithms for efficiency. Replace inefficient loops or data structures with more efficient ones.
- **Reduce Main Thread Load**: Move CPU-intensive tasks off the main thread to background threads or isolates. Use asynchronous patterns (e.g., async/await) to ensure UI responsiveness.
- **Cache Data**: Implement caching strategies to reduce redundant network requests or expensive calculations. Utilize local databases or in-memory caching to store frequently accessed data.
- **Batch Network Requests**: Instead of making multiple individual requests, batch them together when possible to minimize network overhead.

Techniques for Minimizing Memory Usage

Effective memory management is crucial for optimizing performance, especially in resource-constrained mobile environments. Here are techniques to minimize memory usage:

1. **Use Lazy Loading**:

- Load resources only when needed, rather than all at once. This is particularly useful for images, data sets, or complex UI components.

1. **Release Unused Resources**:

- Ensure that objects no longer in use are released promptly. Use weak references where applicable to avoid retaining objects unnecessarily.

1. **Optimize Image and Asset Sizes**:

- Use appropriately sized images and assets for different screen resolutions. Consider using formats that provide compression without sacrificing quality.

1. **Use Memory-efficient Data Structures**:

- Choose data structures that are appropriate for the task at hand. For example, use arrays or linked lists where applicable, and avoid using complex structures unnecessarily.

1. **Profile and Monitor Memory**:

- Regularly profile memory usage during development to identify leaks or areas of high memory consumption. Use tools like Instruments and Memory Profiler to gather insights.

Case Study: Performance Optimization in a Real-World App

Scenario: A mobile app for food delivery that allows users to browse restaurants, place orders, and track deliveries. The app initially experienced slow loading times, unresponsive UI during network requests, and excessive memory usage leading to crashes.

Step 1: Profiling and Analysis

Using **Instruments** (iOS) and **Android Profiler** (Android), the development team performed the following analyses:

- **CPU Analysis**: Found that several UI-related methods were blocking the main thread during data fetching.
- **Memory Analysis**: Detected memory leaks caused by retained view controllers and unoptimized image loading.
- **Network Analysis**: Identified that multiple network requests were being made sequentially, resulting in long loading times.

Step 2: Implementing Optimizations

Based on the profiling data, the team implemented the following optimizations:

1. **Asynchronous Data Fetching**:

- Used background threads to fetch restaurant data and order details, ensuring that the UI remained responsive. Implemented async/await in Swift and coroutines in Kotlin for cleaner asynchronous code.

1. **Image Caching**:

- Implemented an image caching mechanism to store downloaded images locally, reducing redundant network requests. Utilized libraries like SDWebImage for iOS and Glide for Android.

1. **Batching Network Requests**:

- Combined multiple API requests into single batched requests where feasible. This reduced the overhead of making individual calls and improved loading times.

1. **Memory Management**:

- Conducted a code review to ensure proper release of resources and used profiling tools to track memory allocation. Reduced the use of large in-memory data structures and opted for lightweight models.

Step 3: Testing and Validation

After implementing the optimizations, the team conducted extensive testing:

- **Regression Testing**: Ensured that new changes did not break existing functionality.
- **Performance Testing**: Re-profiled the application using Instruments and Android Profiler to validate improvements in CPU usage, memory consumption, and network latency.

Results

- **Improved Loading Times**: Application loading times decreased significantly, enhancing user experience.
- **Responsive UI**: The app became responsive during network requests, reducing user frustration.
- **Lower Memory Usage**: Memory consumption was optimized, leading to fewer crashes and better overall stability.

Performance Optimization and Concurrency

Optimizing the performance of mobile applications is essential for providing users with a smooth and responsive experience. Performance issues, particularly those related to concurrency, can lead to sluggishness, high memory usage, and poor user engagement. This guide covers profiling tools for iOS and Android, techniques for detecting and fixing performance bottlenecks, methods for minimizing memory usage, and a case study demonstrating performance optimization in a real-world application.

Profiling Tools for iOS and Android

Profiling tools allow developers to analyze their applications' performance, identify bottlenecks, and optimize resource usage effectively.

1. **Profiling Tools for iOS (Instruments)**

Instruments is a powerful performance analysis and profiling tool bundled with Xcode. It provides various templates to profile different aspects of an application, including CPU usage, memory allocation, network activity, and more.

Key Instruments for Profiling:

- **Time Profiler**: Measures the CPU usage and helps identify functions that consume significant processing time.
- **Allocations**: Tracks memory usage and object allocation, allowing developers to identify memory leaks and excessive memory consumption.
- **Activity Monitor**: Displays real-time statistics about the app's resource usage, including CPU and memory consumption.
- **Network**: Monitors network activity to analyze requests, data received, and overall network performance.

Example Usage:

1. Open Instruments from Xcode.
2. Select a profiling template (e.g., Time Profiler).
3. Run your app and interact with it to simulate real usage.
4. Analyze the recorded data to identify performance bottlenecks.

2. Profiling Tools for Android (Android Profiler)

Android Profiler is integrated into Android Studio and provides a suite of tools for monitoring an app's performance in real-time.

Key Profiling Features:

- **CPU Profiler**: Visualizes CPU activity, showing which threads are running and what methods are consuming the most CPU time.
- **Memory Profiler**: Tracks memory allocation, allowing developers to identify leaks and memory consumption patterns.
- **Network Profiler**: Monitors network requests, showing request/response times and data transfer details.

Example Usage:

1. Open Android Studio and launch the app in debug mode.
2. Navigate to the Profiler tab.
3. Select the relevant profiler (CPU, Memory, Network) and interact with

the app to gather data.

4. Analyze the recorded data to pinpoint performance issues.

Detecting and Fixing Performance Bottlenecks

Detecting and fixing performance bottlenecks is critical for ensuring smooth app performance. Here are common strategies for identifying and resolving issues:

1. **Identifying Bottlenecks**

- **Analyze CPU Usage**: Use profiling tools to check which methods consume the most CPU resources. Look for long-running tasks, especially those running on the main thread.
- **Monitor Memory Usage**: Identify memory spikes or leaks that could affect performance. High memory consumption can lead to increased garbage collection or even crashes.
- **Profile Network Activity**: Check network latency and data transfer times. Poor network performance can lead to slow data fetching and affect the user experience.

2. **Fixing Bottlenecks**

- **Optimize Algorithms**: Review and optimize algorithms for efficiency. Replace inefficient loops or data structures with more efficient ones.
- **Reduce Main Thread Load**: Move CPU-intensive tasks off the main thread to background threads or isolates. Use asynchronous patterns (e.g., async/await) to ensure UI responsiveness.
- **Cache Data**: Implement caching strategies to reduce redundant network requests or expensive calculations. Utilize local databases or in-memory caching to store frequently accessed data.
- **Batch Network Requests**: Instead of making multiple individual requests, batch them together when possible to minimize network overhead.

Techniques for Minimizing Memory Usage

Effective memory management is crucial for optimizing performance, especially in resource-constrained mobile environments. Here are techniques to minimize memory usage:

1. **Use Lazy Loading**:

- Load resources only when needed, rather than all at once. This is particularly useful for images, data sets, or complex UI components.

1. **Release Unused Resources**:

- Ensure that objects no longer in use are released promptly. Use weak references where applicable to avoid retaining objects unnecessarily.

1. **Optimize Image and Asset Sizes**:

- Use appropriately sized images and assets for different screen resolutions. Consider using formats that provide compression without sacrificing quality.

1. **Use Memory-efficient Data Structures**:

- Choose data structures that are appropriate for the task at hand. For example, use arrays or linked lists where applicable, and avoid using complex structures unnecessarily.

1. **Profile and Monitor Memory**:

- Regularly profile memory usage during development to identify leaks or areas of high memory consumption. Use tools like Instruments and Memory Profiler to gather insights.

Case Study: Performance Optimization in a Real-World App

Scenario: A mobile app for food delivery that allows users to browse restaurants, place orders, and track deliveries. The app initially experienced slow loading times, unresponsive UI during network requests, and excessive memory usage leading to crashes.

Step 1: Profiling and Analysis

Using **Instruments** (iOS) and **Android Profiler** (Android), the development team performed the following analyses:

- **CPU Analysis**: Found that several UI-related methods were blocking the main thread during data fetching.
- **Memory Analysis**: Detected memory leaks caused by retained view controllers and unoptimized image loading.
- **Network Analysis**: Identified that multiple network requests were being made sequentially, resulting in long loading times.

Step 2: Implementing Optimizations

Based on the profiling data, the team implemented the following optimizations:

1. **Asynchronous Data Fetching**:

- Used background threads to fetch restaurant data and order details, ensuring that the UI remained responsive. Implemented async/await in Swift and coroutines in Kotlin for cleaner asynchronous code.

1. **Image Caching**:

- Implemented an image caching mechanism to store downloaded images locally, reducing redundant network requests. Utilized libraries like SDWebImage for iOS and Glide for Android.

1. **Batching Network Requests**:

- Combined multiple API requests into single batched requests where feasible. This reduced the overhead of making individual calls and improved loading times.

1. **Memory Management**:

- Conducted a code review to ensure proper release of resources and used profiling tools to track memory allocation. Reduced the use of large in-memory data structures and opted for lightweight models.

Step 3: Testing and Validation

After implementing the optimizations, the team conducted extensive testing:

- **Regression Testing**: Ensured that new changes did not break existing functionality.
- **Performance Testing**: Re-profiled the application using Instruments and Android Profiler to validate improvements in CPU usage, memory consumption, and network latency.

Results

- **Improved Loading Times**: Application loading times decreased significantly, enhancing user experience.
- **Responsive UI**: The app became responsive during network requests, reducing user frustration.
- **Lower Memory Usage**: Memory consumption was optimized, leading to fewer crashes and better overall stability

Deploying and Maintaining Mobile Apps
with Concurrency

Successfully deploying and maintaining mobile applications, particularly those utilizing concurrency features, requires careful planning and execution. This guide covers the essential steps in preparing your app for production, monitoring and maintaining concurrent features after launch, implementing continuous integration and deployment (CI/CD), and ensuring compatibility across different device versions.

Preparing Your App for Production: Concurrency Checklist

Before deploying your mobile application, it's crucial to ensure that your concurrency features are robust, efficient, and secure. Here's a checklist to help you prepare your app for production:

1. **Concurrency Testing**:

- Conduct thorough testing of all asynchronous and concurrent features, including unit tests, integration tests, and UI tests. Validate that the app behaves as expected under load and in different scenarios.

1. **Performance Profiling**:

- Use profiling tools (e.g., Instruments for iOS, Android Profiler) to identify and fix performance bottlenecks. Ensure that your app maintains good performance even under heavy concurrency loads.

1. **Error Handling**:

- Implement comprehensive error handling for all concurrent operations. Ensure that failures in background tasks do not crash the app and that users receive appropriate feedback.

1. **Security Audit**:

- Perform a security audit focusing on concurrency-related vulnerabilities, such as race conditions, deadlocks, and data integrity issues. Review access controls and data protection mechanisms.

1. **Memory Management**:

- Ensure that your app manages memory efficiently, particularly in concurrent scenarios. Use tools to identify memory leaks and optimize memory usage.

1. **User Experience (UX) Considerations**:

- Make sure the user interface is responsive and provides feedback during long-running tasks. Implement loading indicators, progress bars, or placeholders to enhance the user experience.

1. **Documentation**:

- Document your concurrency architecture and any known limitations or considerations for future developers. Include clear guidelines for maintaining and extending concurrency features.

Monitoring and Maintaining Concurrent Features Post-Launch

Once your app is live, continuous monitoring and maintenance of its concurrent features are essential for ensuring optimal performance and user satisfaction.

1. **Set Up Analytics and Monitoring**:

- Use analytics tools to monitor the app's performance in real-time. Track

key metrics such as response times for asynchronous operations, error rates, and user engagement.
- Implement logging for concurrent operations to capture issues that may arise during execution. Use tools like Firebase Crashlytics for crash reporting.

1. **Feedback Mechanisms**:

- Include user feedback mechanisms to report performance issues related to concurrent tasks. Monitor user reviews and support tickets for recurring problems.

1. **Regular Performance Audits**:

- Conduct regular performance audits post-launch. Revisit profiling tools to identify any new bottlenecks or memory issues that may emerge as usage patterns change.

1. **Updating Dependencies**:

- Regularly update libraries and frameworks used for concurrency to ensure you benefit from the latest performance improvements and security patches.

1. **User-Centric Improvements**:

- Based on user feedback and analytics, iterate on concurrent features to improve performance and usability. Optimize network requests, reduce loading times, and refine the overall user experience.

Continuous Integration and Deployment (CI/CD) with Concurrent Features

Implementing CI/CD practices helps automate the deployment process and maintain a high-quality codebase for concurrent features.

1. **Automated Testing**:

- Integrate automated tests for concurrent features into your CI pipeline. Include unit tests, integration tests, and performance tests to validate that new changes do not introduce regressions.

1. **Build Automation**:

- Automate the build process to ensure that every code change is compiled and tested consistently. Use CI tools like Jenkins, CircleCI, or GitHub Actions to automate builds and deployments.

1. **Staging Environment**:

- Create a staging environment that mimics production to test concurrent features before deployment. This allows you to catch issues in a controlled setting.

1. **Gradual Rollouts**:

- Consider using feature flags to enable gradual rollouts of new features. This allows you to monitor performance and user feedback on concurrent features before a full release.

1. **Monitoring Post-Deployment**:

- After deploying updates, monitor the app closely for any issues related to concurrency. Track performance metrics and user feedback to address any emerging problems quickly.

Ensuring Compatibility Across Different Device Versions

Ensuring that your application functions correctly across various device versions is crucial, especially when using concurrency features that may behave differently on different platforms.

1. **Targeting Multiple Versions**:

- Ensure your app targets the appropriate SDK versions for both iOS and Android. Use API levels and version checks to provide backward compatibility while still leveraging modern concurrency features.

1. **Testing Across Devices**:

- Use emulators and physical devices to test your app across different versions and device configurations. Tools like Firebase Test Lab can help automate this process.

1. **Monitoring Platform-Specific Issues**:

- Monitor performance and behavior on specific device versions. Different operating system versions may have different handling of concurrency features, which could lead to platform-specific issues.

1. **Documenting Compatibility**:

- Document known compatibility issues and behaviors for different device versions. This helps in maintaining clarity for future development and troubleshooting.

1. **Handling Deprecations and Changes**:

- Stay informed about deprecated features or changes in concurrency handling in new releases of iOS or Android. Update your code accordingly to ensure ongoing compatibility.

Future Trends in Mobile Concurrency

As mobile application development continues to evolve, so do the techniques and models used to manage concurrency. The increasing complexity of applications, coupled with advances in hardware and cross-platform capabilities, is driving significant innovations in concurrency management. This guide explores the future trends in mobile concurrency, focusing on the evolution of concurrency models, the impact of hardware advances, cross-platform concurrency innovations, and preparations for emerging technologies.

Evolution of Concurrency Models

1. Swift Concurrency

Swift has introduced a new concurrency model that simplifies asynchronous programming, making it more efficient and easier to read. The adoption of **async/await** syntax allows developers to write asynchronous code that looks similar to synchronous code, improving code maintainability.

- **Structured Concurrency**: Swift's concurrency model emphasizes structured concurrency, ensuring that all asynchronous tasks are scoped and their lifetimes managed appropriately. This reduces the risk of resource leaks and improves code reliability.
- **Task and Actor Types**: Swift introduces the concepts of tasks and actors. Tasks represent asynchronous work, while actors provide a way to manage state across multiple threads safely.

Future Implications:

- As Swift continues to evolve, we can expect further enhancements to the concurrency model, making it easier for developers to handle complex asynchronous workflows with better performance and safety.

2. **Kotlin Coroutines**

Kotlin coroutines have become the preferred way to handle asynchronous programming in Android development. They provide a lightweight, non-blocking way to work with concurrency.

- **Structured Concurrency**: Similar to Swift, Kotlin promotes structured concurrency. Coroutine scopes (like viewModelScope and lifecycle-Scope) help manage the lifecycle of coroutines, making them easy to use without risking memory leaks.
- **Flow**: Kotlin introduces Flow, a reactive stream implementation that simplifies handling asynchronous data streams. This makes it easier to handle events like user inputs, database changes, or network responses.

Future Implications:

- With ongoing improvements and adoption, Kotlin coroutines will likely continue to shape asynchronous programming in the Android ecosystem, influencing other JVM languages as well.

Impact of Hardware Advances

Advancements in hardware, particularly multicore processors and GPUs, are significantly affecting how concurrency is implemented in mobile applications.

1. **Multicore Processors**

Modern mobile devices are equipped with multicore processors, allowing for true parallel execution of tasks. This development enables:

- **Increased Performance**: Developers can design applications that leverage multiple cores for concurrent processing, leading to improved performance for CPU-intensive tasks like video rendering or complex calculations.
- **Task Distribution**: Frameworks are evolving to better distribute workloads across available cores. This trend is likely to continue, allowing

for more efficient execution of concurrent tasks.

2. GPUs for Concurrency

Graphics Processing Units (GPUs) are being increasingly utilized for general-purpose computing, including concurrency:

- **GPGPU Computing**: Technologies such as OpenCL and Metal in iOS allow developers to leverage the power of GPUs for concurrent processing tasks. This is particularly useful for image processing, machine learning, and real-time graphics rendering.
- **Improved Graphics Performance**: Enhanced concurrency capabilities in graphics engines lead to smoother animations and transitions, providing a better user experience.

Future Implications:

- As mobile devices continue to advance in hardware capabilities, developers will increasingly leverage multicore and GPU architectures to improve application performance and responsiveness.

Cross-Platform Concurrency Innovations

Cross-platform frameworks are continuously evolving to support concurrency more effectively, enabling developers to build applications that run seamlessly on multiple platforms.

1. Flutter's Isolate Model

Flutter utilizes isolates for concurrent execution. This model allows developers to run Dart code in a separate memory space, making it easy to handle CPU-intensive tasks without blocking the main UI thread.

- **Future Developments**: The Flutter community is actively enhancing its concurrency model. Future updates may introduce new patterns or tools to simplify communication between isolates and improve the developer experience.

2. **React Native Concurrency**

React Native's architecture supports the JavaScript concurrency model, allowing for asynchronous operations using Promises and async/await. With the introduction of features like **Concurrent Mode** in React, developers can build more responsive UIs.

- **Future Innovations**: The React Native ecosystem is expected to continue evolving, focusing on improving the performance of concurrent features and making it easier to integrate native modules that can leverage concurrent processing.

Preparing for the Future: Emerging Technologies and Techniques

To stay ahead in the evolving landscape of mobile concurrency, developers should be aware of emerging technologies and techniques that can enhance their applications:

1. **Machine Learning and AI**:

- As mobile apps increasingly incorporate machine learning and AI features, understanding how to handle concurrent processing for these tasks will be vital. Frameworks like TensorFlow Lite enable efficient model inference on mobile devices, often using concurrency for data processing.

1. **Serverless Architectures**:

- Serverless computing can offload some concurrent processing tasks to the cloud, reducing the load on mobile devices. Understanding how to architect apps to leverage serverless features will become increasingly important.

1. **Reactive Programming**:

- Reactive programming paradigms are gaining popularity for managing asynchronous data streams. Familiarity with frameworks like RxJava, RxSwift, and Kotlin Flow will be beneficial for developers looking to build responsive applications.

1. **Decentralized Applications**:

- With the rise of blockchain and decentralized technologies, understanding how to manage concurrency in distributed applications will become critical. This includes managing data consistency and security across multiple nodes.

1. **Integration with IoT**:

- As mobile devices increasingly connect with IoT devices, managing concurrency for real-time data processing from multiple sensors or devices will be essential.

Case Studies and Real-World Applications

Examining real-world applications of concurrency in mobile development provides valuable insights into best practices and challenges. This section presents three case studies that highlight the implementation of concurrency in different types of applications, followed by lessons learned from these experiences.

Case Study 1: Building a Messaging App with Concurrent Network Operations

Overview

The development of a messaging app (e.g., ChatApp) required efficient handling of concurrent network operations to support features such as real-time message delivery, user presence updates, and media sharing.

Implementation

1. **Concurrency Model**:

- The app utilized **WebSockets** for real-time communication, allowing multiple users to send and receive messages simultaneously.
- Asynchronous HTTP requests were made using **Kotlin coroutines** for Android and **async/await** for iOS to handle API calls for message fetching and sending.

1. **Background Tasks**:

- Background tasks were implemented to sync messages when the app was not in the foreground, using **WorkManager** on Android and **BackgroundTasks** on iOS.
- Push notifications were leveraged to alert users of new messages, ensuring they stayed updated even when the app was not active.

1. **Error Handling**:

- Robust error handling was integrated to manage network failures gracefully. Exponential backoff strategies were employed for retrying failed message sends.

Results

- The app achieved real-time performance with minimal latency in message delivery.
- User engagement increased, as the app effectively notified users of incoming messages and updates.

Case Study 2: Developing a Real-Time Data Analytics App

Overview

This case study focuses on a real-time data analytics app designed to visualize streaming data from various sources, including IoT devices and external APIs.

Implementation

1. **Concurrency Model**:

- The app utilized **Kotlin coroutines** to handle data fetching and processing in parallel. This allowed for multiple data streams to be processed concurrently without blocking the main UI thread.
- **RxJava** was used to create reactive streams for continuous data process-

ing, enabling seamless updates to the UI as new data arrived.

1. **Data Visualization**:

- Charts and graphs were updated in real-time using concurrent operations. The app employed **LiveData** in Android and **Combine** in iOS to reactively update the UI when new data points were available.

1. **Data Caching**:

- A caching mechanism was implemented to store recent data locally, minimizing the need for repeated network requests and improving app responsiveness.

Results

- The app successfully visualized real-time data with high performance and responsiveness.
- Users reported improved decision-making capabilities due to timely insights from streaming data.

Case Study 3: Implementing Concurrency in a Streaming App

Overview

The streaming app aimed to deliver audio and video content to users while maintaining a smooth user experience even under varying network conditions.

Implementation

1. **Concurrency Model**:

- The app employed **AVFoundation** for iOS and **ExoPlayer** for Android to handle media playback. These frameworks are designed to manage playback tasks efficiently in the background.

- Asynchronous preloading techniques were used to buffer content ahead of time, ensuring seamless playback during network fluctuations.

1. **Adaptive Streaming**:

- The app utilized adaptive bitrate streaming to adjust the quality of the media being delivered based on the user's network conditions, ensuring uninterrupted playback.
- The implementation of a custom loading indicator provided feedback during buffering, enhancing the user experience.

1. **Error Handling**:

- Comprehensive error handling mechanisms were incorporated to manage playback interruptions due to network issues. Users were informed of connectivity problems, with options to retry.

Results

- The streaming app delivered high-quality media playback with minimal interruptions, even on slower connections.
- User feedback highlighted the effectiveness of the adaptive streaming feature and the responsive UI.

Lessons Learned from Real-World App Development

1. **Embrace Asynchronous Programming**:

- Utilizing asynchronous programming models (such as async/await and coroutines) significantly simplifies code and improves app responsiveness. It allows developers to write cleaner, more maintainable code without deeply nested callbacks.

1. **Prioritize User Experience**:

- Ensure that user experience remains at the forefront of concurrency implementations. Provide feedback during long-running tasks, and handle errors gracefully to maintain user trust and engagement.

1. **Thorough Testing is Essential**:

- Testing for concurrency issues (e.g., race conditions, deadlocks) is crucial. Implement comprehensive automated tests that cover various concurrency scenarios to catch issues early in development.

1. **Monitor and Optimize Performance**:

- Continuously monitor app performance post-launch. Use profiling tools to identify bottlenecks and optimize concurrency handling to improve responsiveness and resource usage.

1. **Implement Robust Error Handling**:

- Robust error handling mechanisms are necessary to manage network failures and other concurrency-related issues. Strategies like exponential backoff for retries can enhance the user experience.

1. **Stay Informed on Best Practices**:

- The field of concurrency in mobile app development is constantly evolving. Staying updated on the latest frameworks, tools, and best practices is essential for maintaining high-quality applications

Conclusion

The landscape of mobile app development is continually evolving, and managing concurrency effectively is crucial for building responsive, high-performance applications. This conclusion summarizes key concepts and techniques, outlines future learning pathways, recommends resources and communities, and offers final thoughts on mobile app development and concurrency.

Recap of Key Concepts and Techniques

1. **Concurrency Models**:

- Understanding different concurrency models, such as **async/await**, **Kotlin coroutines**, and **reactive programming** with **RxJava/RxSwift**, is fundamental for developing responsive applications.
- Emphasis on **structured concurrency** helps maintain clear lifecycles for asynchronous tasks, reducing the risk of memory leaks and making code easier to manage.

1. **Concurrency in Mobile Frameworks**:

- **Swift Concurrency** introduces powerful constructs like Task and Actor, simplifying asynchronous programming in iOS.
- **Kotlin Coroutines** provide a lightweight mechanism to manage concurrency, ensuring seamless integration with Android applications.

1. **Performance Optimization**:

- Profiling tools (e.g., Instruments for iOS, Android Profiler) are essential for identifying performance bottlenecks in concurrent applications.
- Techniques like lazy loading, caching, and efficient memory management contribute to enhancing app performance.

1. **Security Considerations**:

- Protecting data integrity and privacy in multithreaded environments is vital. Using thread-safe data structures, encryption, and proper error handling mitigates risks associated with concurrency.
- Safeguarding against race conditions and concurrency attacks requires diligent coding practices and thorough testing.

1. **Real-World Applications**:

- Case studies demonstrate practical applications of concurrency in messaging apps, data analytics apps, and streaming services, highlighting best practices and lessons learned.

Future Learning Pathways

1. **Advanced Concurrency Topics**:

- Explore advanced concurrency patterns such as **actor models**, **message passing**, and **parallel programming** concepts.
- Delve into performance optimization techniques specific to mobile environments, including GPU programming and machine learning model deployment.

1. **Emerging Technologies**:

- Stay informed about emerging technologies like **serverless architecture**, **edge computing**, and **decentralized applications** that may impact concurrency strategies.

1. **Cross-Platform Development**:

- Gain expertise in cross-platform frameworks (e.g., Flutter, React Native) to understand how concurrency is managed across different platforms.

1. **Continuous Learning**:

- Engage in online courses, workshops, and conferences focused on mobile development, concurrency, and related technologies.

Recommended Resources and Communities

1. **Books**:

- *Concurrency in Swift* by Gwendolyn S. D. F.
- *Kotlin Coroutines by Tutorials* from raywenderlich.com
- *Reactive Programming with RxJava* by Ben Christensen

1. **Online Courses**:

- Udacity's courses on Android development and concurrency.
- Coursera's courses on mobile app development and reactive programming.
- Pluralsight's training on Swift and Kotlin concurrency.

1. **Communities**:

- Join forums and communities such as Stack Overflow, Reddit (e.g., r/iOSProgramming, r/androiddev), and the Swift and Kotlin Slack groups to engage with other developers.
- Participate in GitHub repositories focused on mobile concurrency projects to learn from practical examples and contribute.

1. **Meetups and Conferences**:

- Attend local or virtual meetups focused on mobile development, where you can learn from industry experts and network with peers.

- Look for conferences like WWDC (Apple), Google I/O, and KotlinConf, which cover the latest developments in mobile app technology.

Final Thoughts on Mobile App Development and Concurrency

M obile app development continues to be a dynamic field where concurrency plays a crucial role in enhancing user experience and app performance. As mobile devices become increasingly powerful and capable of running more complex applications, the importance of efficient concurrency management will only grow.

Embracing modern concurrency models, adhering to best practices, and continuously learning about new tools and techniques will empower developers to create robust, high-performance applications. By focusing on optimizing performance, ensuring security, and understanding user needs, developers can build applications that not only meet but exceed expectations.